SHAKESPEARE: A TEACHER'S HANDBOOK

Wendy Michaels

Jesse Hise

Ken Watson

Anthony Adams

ACKNOWLEDGEMENTS

The authors would like to thank The Shakespeare Globe Centre Australia Inc for permission to include material that first appeared in its brochures.

Portions of Part A were first published in *When The Hurly Burly Is Done* by Wendy Michaels (Sydney: St Clair Press, 1986).

The material in Part B was originally published in *Shakespeare Festival* by Jesse Hise (Lakeside, California: Interact, 1993).

The authors are grateful for the many suggestions for teaching Shakespeare's plays which have come from Brenda Pinder and other authors in the St Clair *Shakespeare workshop Series*.

ISBN 1 876757 03 5

St Clair Press

Shakespeare: A Teacher's Handbook is published by St Clair Press
an imprint of PHOENIX EDUCATION PTY LTD

Sydney
PO Box 3141, Putney 2112
Tel: (02) 9809 3579 Fax: (02) 9808 1430

Melbourne
PO Box 197, Albert Park 3206
Tel: (03) 9699 8377 Fax: (03) 9699 9242

Email: service@phoenixeduc.com
Website: www.phoenixeduc.com

© 2001 Wendy Michaels, Jesse Hise, Ken Watson, Anthony Adams
First published 1994. Reprinted with corrections and additions 1995, 1997.
Second edition 2001. Reprinted 2003

PHOTOCOPYING

CONTENTS

Abbreviations

In this book the following abbreviations refer to volumes
in the *Shakespeare Workshop Series*:

AC	*Gaze on Cleopatra: Antony and Cleopatra*
AYL	*Love's Keen Arrows: As You Like It*
HAM	*A Workshop Approach to Hamlet*
HIV	*The Theme of Honour's Tongue: Henry IV, Part I*
HV	*We Happy Few: Henry V*
JC	*The Dogs Of War: Julius Caesar*
KL	*Sharper Than A Serpent's Tooth: King Lear*
MA	*A Skirmish Of Wit: Much Ado About Nothing*
MAC	*Creative Work Ideas for Macbeth*
MM	*Some by Virtue Fall: Measure for Measure*
MND	*The Course of True Love: A Midsummer Night's Dream*
MSS	*A Dagger of the Mind: Macbeth for Senior Students*
MV	*Let Him Look to His Bond: The Merchant of Venice*
MWW	*Moonshine Revellers: The Merry Wives of Windsor*
OTH	*The Green-Ey'd Monster: Othello*
RIII	*To Prove A Villain: Richard III*
RJ	*Star-Cross'd Lovers: Romeo and Juliet*
RWT	*Bitter Bread: Richard II* and *The Winter's Tale* ·
TEM	*Full Fathom Five: The Tempest*
TN	*The Food of Love: Twelfth Night*
TS	*Such a Mad Marriage: The Taming of the Shrew*

INTRODUCTION

When the first edition of *Shakespeare: A Teacher's Handbook* was published in 1994, it was assumed that the St Clair *Shakespeare Workshop Series*, which the *Handbook* was intended to complement, was now complete. In succeeding years, however, several more of Shakespeare's plays have found their way into the school curriculum, particularly at senior level, thus necessitating a revision. In addition, valuable new resources (including internet websites) have become available.

This new edition of the *Handbook* leaves the first three chapters and Part B unchanged, but additions have been made to Chapter 3 and to Part C , adding further activities, incorporating cross-references to the newer titles in the Shakespeare *Workshop Series and* greatly expanding the lists of resource materials and references. Teachers will find the section 'Shakespeare and the New Technologies', compiled by Anthony Adams of Cambridge University, a particularly valuable feature, as it details some of the most valuable resources available on the internet and gives particulars of CD-ROMs on Shakespearian plays. The philosophy behind the series may be summed up as follows:

1. Students should see the text in front of them, not as the play, but as a *playscript* that must be turned into a play.

2. They should be invited to engage, in groups, in a range of activities which constantly require them to think in dramatic, theatrical terms. The activities place them in roles of director, scene designer, and actors creating a play from the blueprint provided by Shakespeare.

As well as providing valuable background material on Shakespeare's theatre, the *Handbook* offers a range of practical suggestions to help teachers present Shakespeare in this active way.

In addition, there is a lengthy section by Jesse Hise on running your own Shakespeare Festival. Some years ago Jesse received a generous grant from the US. Office of Education to develop a Shakespeare Festival in his school. The Festival is now an annual event, and Jesse's immensely practical account will encourage teachers in other countries to do likewise.

Ken Watson

Twelfth Night, *Act 2 scene 5: Malvolio soliloquising.*
Engraving by C Heath after the painting by J M Wright.

PART A
Shakespeare In
The Classroom

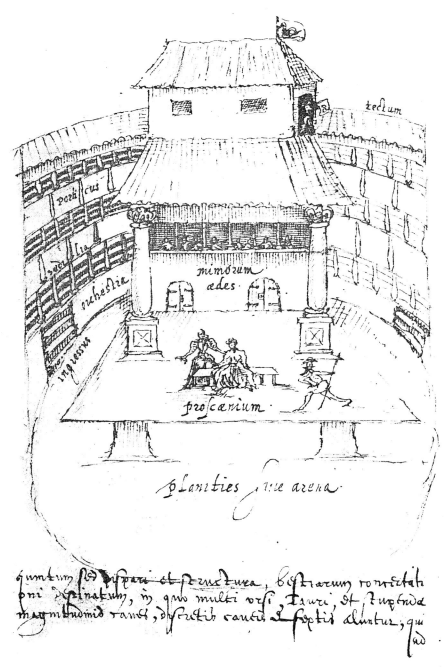

tectum

porticus

orchestra

mimorum
aedes

ingressus

proscænium

planties sive arena

De Witt's drawing of the Swan Theatre, c.1596

CHAPTER 1:
PLOTS HAVE I LAID ...

Wendy Michaels

Among English teachers there has been considerable debate as to the relevance, usefulness and practicality of including Shakespeare in the classroom program. Many English teachers feel uncomfortable teaching play scripts as "drama". Some lack the requisite knowledge of drama and theatre to teach the plays as scripts for performance. Consequently, they tend to avoid using drama scripts in their programs, or include them but treat them as another kind of novel. Shakespeare poses greater problems for them than other playscripts, because the language seems difficult and the plot is far from linear. Other teachers argue that Shakespeare has little relevance for students who come from non-Anglo cultures, and that the language is too difficult for students for whom English is a second language.

Of those English teachers who do include Shakespeare in their programs, many subscribe to the "cultural heritage" model of English. All students today need to be taught the best that has been thought and written in English, so that they may be ennobled and enlightened, and may come to understand the basis of their cultural heritage. Shakespeare, they would argue, is the greatest writer in the canons of English, having produced the finest poetry ever written. Contemporary students should study his works so that they can understand and appreciate the best of English Literature.

I do not propose to enter into debating these issues, merely to state them as the context within which I make my propositions. In passing, however, I would like to say that the Schools Festival organised by The Shakespeare Globe Centre Australia appears to be revitalising interest in exploring Shakespeare's plays in classrooms, by playing down the cultural heritage model and focusing on the plays performed.

It is a truism that the experience of "reading" a printed playscript differs from the experience of "reading" a performed play. Obviously, in the latter case the visual impact is realised in the physical presence of actors and all the trappings of the theatre – and much of the meaning of a play is contained in what the audience sees. More importantly, there are similarities between the way we read a performed play and the way we read other printed narratives, for instance, in the ways we position ourselves in relation to the story, are drawn into following the line of action and empathising with some characters while rejecting or condemning others. Our responses may also be mediated by the obvious responses of other members of the audience with whom we are sharing the experience of "reading" the performed play. This mode of reading has been called by Louise Rosenblatt (1987) "aesthetic" reading.

While it is possible to read a printed playscript in this way, particularly if only the dialogue is read, it is my contention that the playscript form demands a different mode of reading for its meanings to be fully realised. A playscript is, essentially, a blueprint for production. It is a set of instructions to actors, directors, and designers, for the physical realisation in a performance space. Ingarden (1973) has used the terms *Haupttext* and *Nebentext* to distinguish the dialogue which the actors speak, and any directions in the form of narrative or description which frame the dialogue the actors speak, and any directions in the form of narrative or description which frame the dialogue. Aston and Savona (1991) cite Veltrusky who makes a further distinction between instructions that are extradialogic and those which are intradialogic. Instructions which are extradialogic, that is explicitly stated in the text, may take the form of detailed descriptions of aspects of the set or characters (eg. *Downstage R is a large, padded armchair covered with a pink and mauve floral patterned fabric*), or in the case of Miller's *The Crucible*, extensive pieces of exposition; or they may simply be single words interpolated in the dialogue as an instruction to an actor as to how to speak or move, (eg. *Sadly*, or, *Pause*).

Intradialogic instructions are those which are implicit in the dialogue ("Be these tears wet?") This latter is, of course, usually the case in Shakespeare's scripts. Aston and Savona (1991) assert, "The text itself ... states the terms of its own staging." Printed playscripts, whether containing extradialogic or intradialogic stage directions, may be seen as falling into the category of "procedural texts". They tell the reader how the play might be realised in production. As such they require a mode of reading that differs from "aesthetic" reading; they require a mode that allows the reader to stand outside the text and extricate from it the information required, and from this information to visualise what is happening on the stage. This mode of reading has been called "efferent" reading (Rosenblatt, 1987).

Reading in this way is quite a different notion from the reading of subtext which Arnold (1987) describes. She is essentially working from a model that seeks to evoke "webs of personal response" to the words on the page, reading them as if they were the real speech of real characters, rather than instructions to an actor in a play. Such a reading, while valuable at one level, does not access the intradialogic directions that are embedded in Shakespeare's text.

Despite Hayman's (1977) contention that Shakespeare gave "very little information in stage directions", Styan (1977) has amply demonstrated that in Shakespeare's plays the instructions are embedded in the lines spoken by actors. These instructions are not merely indicators of how to speak the speech, but also of the kinesics and proxemics of the performance. The implicit instructions may not be evident until the words are translated into action on a large thrust stage such as the one for which Shakespeare wrote.

Being able to read these texts efferently will assist students to gain access to the information that is embedded in them. For the contemporary student the process of reading may be complicated by the attempts of editors to provide extradialogic stage directions that may be inappropriate, or even inaccurate, such as the edition of *Antony and Cleopatra* in which the stage direction appended to Enobarbus' death asserts that he stabs himself!

Lack of familiarity with text form impedes a reader's ability to construct meaning from a text. Both Unsworth (1985) and Bartlett (1985) have dealt with the problem of students' reading of text forms that are unfamiliar or unusually complex. Meek (1989) has demonstrated "How Texts Teach What Readers Learn". The text structures and linguistic forms of Shakespeare's plays are complex and diverse, and for many students may be an impediment to reading. This problem is often expressed in a statement about the language being difficult, (always, however, spoken with a tone of reverence and awe), and all too often the focus shifts to obsolete words and phrases. But this is not the real source of the difficulty – rather it lies in the unusual discourse structures of the procedural text, which require a different mode of reading.

Reading a procedural text does not depend so much on reading to discover what occurs next, but rather how it occurs. It is my contention that by enabling students to shift the focus from reading for story to reading for action – that is a shift from reading to find out what happens next, to reading to find out how it happens – we are assisting them to read the printed playscripts efferently. It seems to me that a pre-requisite for this is to ensure that students have some knowledge of the narrative before reading the text.

A second premise underpinning my position derives from the notion of context. Shakespeare's plays were written and performed in a particular cultural, social and theatrical context. In one sense we can never truly know that context. The best we can do is a reconstruction of the values, ideologies and social relationships that we believe to have been part of that context. Our reconstruction will, of course, be shaped by our own set of values. Bradley's (1904) vision of the essence of Shakespearian Tragedy as being "pre-eminently the story of one person" is an obvious example of this. Our reconstruction of the theatrical context may bring us closer to the plays – and we await with interest the reconstructed Globe Theatre at Bankside to test this premise further.

Every reconstruction is, of course, a product of a new context, and this is true of each reconstruction, each new production, of the plays themselves. There never can be a definitive *Hamlet, Othello, Macbeth* or *Shrew*. Each new performance brings to the play a new set of cultural, social and theatrical values and practices. This is epitomised in the way we talk of Mel Gibson's *Hamlet*, Olivier's *Othello*, Polanski's *Macbeth* or Elizabeth Taylor's *Shrew*.

This situation poses problems for educationists – whose plays are our students to study? My quick answer would be **all** versions, but of course, that is not practicable in most situations. Let me put it another way, the one I would not want them to study is the one reconstructed by the literary critic who does not understand how the plays work on a large, bare thrust stage.

This problem is further compounded by the discrepancies between folio and quarto editions, and by editors who have presented differing views of what the correct words on the page must be. The notion that there is a single correct version, of course, assumes that Shakespeare, or his actors, made no revisions of the once-written text during the rehearsal process or during a production run. With Shakespeare's company working in collaborative ensemble, it seems implausible that rewrites and reworkings did not occur. I am rather fond of the story that suggests that the line which Hotspur speaks in *Henry IV Part I* when he enters with the conspirators, "Zounds, I forgot the map" was an interpolation by an actor who entered without his prop! True or not, it illustrates the point that there is simply not one, single, correct version of each play. The alternate endings of *King Lear* provide another obvious example of this, as does the alternate *Hamlet*, which has the memorable line – "To be or not to be. Aye that's the point".

The collaborative ensemble mode of working replicates the ideal learning situation for the drama classroom. Central to drama curricula in Australia (and explicitly expressed in the 2 Unit Drama Syllabus produced by the NSW Board of Studies, 1990) is the principle of experiential learning. Experiential learning implies a collaborative and interactive process where learners participate in workshop situations, engaging in active exploration and in reflection on the activities.

There has been some discussion as to the nature and importance of "practical work". The term "practical" is an unfortunate one – often used to imply something antithetical to theoretical, and by implication, not engaging cognitive processes. I want to draw a distinction between the type of practical activity that is nothing more than "busyness", directionless, unstructured, "fun" activity, and the type of practical activity that challenges students to engage in a problem solving situation using physical, affective and cognitive capacities. This type of practical work is structured so that students achieve worthwhile learning outcomes, while still having "fun".

The role of the teacher in such classrooms requires a flexibility that may not be needed in other styles of classroom. The teacher will adopt roles of differing stance and differing status. At times the teacher may use roles within the workshop activity, at other times the role will be outside the activity. Such variation in teacher roles also implies a variation in student roles. These roles may include the roles of theatre practitioners, characters within a playscript, "mantle of the expert" or other roles outside these parameters.

Whatever the roles or the specific nature of the activity these elements will be discernible:
- collaboration and co-operation
- interaction and exploration
- negotiation and contribution
- experimentation and resolution
- presentation and response
- consolidation and discussion
- reflection.

Preserving the integrity of this style of learning environment in the current education climate can be a problem. One of the pressures that tends to cause teachers to cave in has come from the outcomes-based education movement which demands quality control and a productivity push. For many teachers this has been the last straw in a narrowing of curriculum, and a consequent strangling of classroom practice.

While outcomes-based education may have had its inception in the economic rationalist push for productivity, accountability and quality control, it may well have some very positive outcomes for the teaching of drama and the teaching of Shakespeare in particular. When all the political paraphernalia has been peeled back, outcomes-based education poses three quintessential questions:

- What do we want students to know and understand?
- What do we want students to be able to do?
- What do we want students to value?

By confronting these questions we can make decisions not only about the content of curricula, but also about methodologies and strategies to be employed in the implementation of these curricula. Making these decisions also makes us put our own value system "up front".

There are obviously many possible answers to these questions, and each set of answers will reveal a particular ideological viewpoint. I offer you now my own answers to these questions in relation to the teaching of Shakespeare's plays – and in doing so, will reveal my own ideology. I will concentrate on answering the first question, and in doing so will provide answers to the second and third. It seems to me that whatever it is we want students to value, stems from what we want them to know and understand, but more importantly it will determine and direct the methodology and teaching strategies to be used in the implementation of the curriculum, and therefore determine the skills that can be acquired.

In answer to the first question, I would want students to know and understand:

- about themselves as human beings and their interpersonal relationships with others – **a psychodynamic dimension;**

- about the cultural/social context which they, and others inhabit – **a sociocultural dimension;**

- about the aesthetics of theatre art, including printed and performed texts – **an aesthetic dimension.**

In the process of gaining this knowledge and understanding, students will develop skills in reading, thinking and feeling, and will learn to value Shakespeare's plays as cultural and aesthetic artefacts, and to value their own personal responses to and interpretations of the plays.

The achieving of these skills and values outcomes determines the methodology to be used in implementing a curriculum involving Shakespeare's works. I have already outlined the general parameters of such a methodology. I turn now to the specific features. I mentioned earlier in my proposition that students are assisted in their reading of the plays by a knowledge of the narrative. I am not suggesting summaries of each act, or detailed study of *Lamb's Tales*. Rather I would suggest the use of active drama-in-education strategies that allow students to engage with the narrative. I mention three such strategies:

- Teacher as narrator tells story in outline. Students in groups present their response to the narrative using depictions, freeze frames or storyboard.

- Teacher in role as a main character takes the hot seat and answers students' questions about incidents, events and other characters.

- Students in groups are presented with key lines from the play that trace the main events. Students use the lines to create an "instant play".

In the psychodynamic dimension we are seeking to facilitate individual students' connection with the characters in the plays. The primary aim is to tap into students' own visions of themselves and their relations with others and to connect these with their responses to the characters in the plays. Essentially we are asking them to consider which characters they like or admire, and which they dislike or condemn, which characters they empathise with and which they reject; and to identify how they might have reacted in the same situation as these characters, or how they might interact with these characters.

To achieve these learning outcomes we might begin with strategies such as parallel improvisations of scenes, incidents or events that characters in the play are involved in. Thus, students might explore through parallel improvisations a situation of feuding gangs prior to exploring the opening scene of *Romeo & Juliet*. Or, they might explore scenes of an elderly man sorting out his will and dividing his fortune among his progeny before beginning an exploration of *King Lear*. Parallel improvisations can also be used to explore characters reactions after explorations of scenes.

Depiction of key moments is another useful device to assist students in connecting with characters, and particularly with the interactions and interpersonal relationships between characters. Students may be given the scenario for particular moments in a play prior to reading the play. They construct depictions for these moments which are then "read" by the watchers/audience. These readings may be expanded and elaborated through the use of captioning, thought balloons or speech bubbles being added to the depictions, or through using a voices-off technique (see Michaels 1991).

Depictions can also be used to construct segments of the text in sequence as demonstrated in Michaels (1992). Freeze frames may be developed from the depictions, and some of the techniques that Boal (1992) uses in his Forum Theatre may be adapted to this use of depiction. The depiction may snap into action, members of the audience may freeze the action and step in to replace a character and attempt to resolve the moment in a different way. Thus, for instance, a depiction of the banquet scene in *Macbeth* might find a number of students exploring differing responses from Macbeth or Lady Macbeth to the ghost's presence.

Other strategies that also assist students to connect with characters include speaking diaries, alter ego, and hot seat. In each of these activities, the character's motivation is explored from different perspectives. Writing in the role of a character also encourages student's identification and empathy with characters.

But I must sound a word of warning at this point. I am not advocating a psychological critical framework as the basis of understanding of the plays. On the contrary, I would argue that to adopt such a critical perspective is to ignore or distort the non-naturalistic form of the play and leads to such misrepresentations as the presentation of the soliloquy as an interior monologue, rather than a dialogue between character and audience.

The sociocultural dimension of study involves an exploration of the structures, mores and ideologies of the plays' worlds, and the making of comparisons with students' own world views. By examining the value system of the plays' worlds students are able to clarify their own value systems.

In encouraging students to explore the structures of the play, we may use techniques that assist them to establish the power relationships in the play. Various mapping and charting techniques, particularly sociograms, are useful here. Students should be encouraged to develop and present these in visual as well as verbal forms.

In establishing the mores of the play's world students could be encouraged to use a variety of role positions outside the text. For instance, the use of mantle-of-the-expert role can be readily exploited here in a way demonstrated by Hughes (1992). Students can be enrolled as cultural anthropologists exploring the cultural practices of Rome and Egypt as they are revealed in *Antony and Cleopatra*.

Other roles outside the play may include roles of theatre practitioners. The dramaturge role is particularly useful here. In this role students explore the mores as revealed in the play with information gathered from other research. The result of this research might be presented in the form of program notes designed to assist an audience connect with the world of the play. Similarly role situations may assist students in identifying and articulating the ideology of the play. This might be stated in a manifesto such as a Desiderata.

To me, the aesthetic dimension is the most significant one for the teaching of any play, but particularly Shakespeare's plays, for it marks the point where students come to understand the play as a construct, an artefact, a crafted and wrought work of art.

To assist students in understanding the plays as wrought artefacts we need to ensure that they do read the plays efferently as well as aesthetically. We can do so by structuring the context of the reading. There are two aspects of such structuring – the role that students adopt as readers, and the contextual framing that we construct for the reading. I spoke earlier of the need for flexibility of roles. At this point I would propose that the most significant reader roles are those related to the practice of theatre, such as actor, director, designer, dramaturge. By framing the context I am suggesting that students be required to read in the nominated role for a specific purpose related to one of three types of framing:
- theatre/stage frame
- structure/form frame
- semiotic frame.

By theatre/stage framing I am suggesting that students focus on the physical realities of the theatre and stage for which Shakespeare wrote, and read the scripts with the specific focus of establishing how the words on the page might have been transformed into action on a stage. To do this, students will require some knowledge of the parameters of the stage and theatre in Elizabethan and Jacobean England. I am not suggesting a detailed study of stage history – but rather an understanding of how a large, open, bare, thrust stage works, with its two doors as entrances, lack of scenery, balcony at the back, and the nature of the relationship that was possible between the actors and audience.

The problem may then be posed to the students to read the playscripts with the specific task of determining how they worked in this space. To do so students may use blocking plans, depictions, or other rehearsal techniques appropriate to the reader roles assigned. Thus, for instance, they might explore through blocking plans, the opening scene of *Antony and Cleopatra* to discover how the use of onstage audience works, and to assist in visualising the images of following and leading that are essential to an understanding of the rest of this play.

The opening scene of *Romeo and Juliet* or the murder scene from *Macbeth* might be explored using a series of depictions or freeze frames in this large space, to make evident the use of the two doors and to show how these take on a symbolic significance – In *Romeo and Juliet* each door becomes associated with either the Capulets or Montagues, and in *Macbeth* with the harrowing of the Gates of Hell.

Through reading that is framed in this way, students will discover the way in which the bare stage makes evident the social and power relationships between characters through the proxemics of the space. The first meeting of Antony and Caesar in Act 2 of *Antony and Cleopatra* will be seen as a power struggle expressed through the space and positioning on the stage.

This theatre/stage framing also assists students to explore the use of dual action in scenes such as the forest scenes in *A Midsummer Night's Dream,* or the use of play-within-a-play in a number of plays, precisely because it asks them to explore where the characters might be positioned on the stage and then to read from this the ideas of the scene.

It also allows students to explore the use of soliloquy as a dialogue between actor/character and audience. This is particularly important, I believe, as the use of soliloquy is often perceived, in this post Freudian world, as an interior monologue, a character speaking to him/herself, inadvertently revealing id impulses. To read the soliloquies thus is to give a different meaning to them. I am not prepared to say that this is a wrong reading – merely a different one which can change the perception that the audience has of the character. Perhaps one of the best examples of this is the "honour" soliloquy that Falstaff speaks in *Henry IV Part 1*. This soliloquy contains a number of questions – "What is Honour?" and answers to these – "A word". If we read this soliloquy as an interior monologue made audible, we can, perhaps, reject Falstaff's logic and dismiss him as a coward. If we, as audience, interact in this speech, providing the answers to his questions, then we have been complicit in assisting Falstaff to his conclusions – and we are therefore less likely to condemn him as a coward.

In providing students with a structural framing for their reading we are encouraging them to look closely at the form to determine the patterns in the dialogue and action. I am not merely meaning verbal images - in fact, on the contrary, I want students to see structural patterns that emerge from the placement of soliloquy, monologue, duologue or dialogue, from single focus action, dual action, onstage audience, play-within the play, aside; from prose, blank verse, heroic couplet; and from the use of caesura, enjambment and verse lining.

In exploring the play from this perspective we may reinforce the notion of the play as artefact, and begin to see patterns that create meanings for the audience. These patterns are particularly important in positioning the audience in terms of the play's ideology. We are asking the students to consider from the point of view of the audience, how the patterns of action may pattern the play's meaning.

Again, some background knowledge of the general effects of soliloquy, monologue, duologue is needed by the students before they can assign significance to the way that Iago's soliloquies often follow a duologue where he has duped Roderigo, Othello or Cassio. The question to be asked is: Where does this patterning place the audience?

Similarly, in exploring patterns of prose, blank verse and heroic couplet, students can come to understand the rhythm, pace, tone and movement of the play. The notion that the prose is spoken by less important characters while blank verse is the province of the main characters can be immediately dispelled as students discover the dramatic function of Enobarbus' prose lines interspersed with the blank verse of Antony and Caesar in Act 2 Scene 2 of *Antony and Cleopatra* juxtaposed with the burnished barge verse monologue later in the scene.

And again, exploring Shakespeare's use of caesura, enjambment and verse lining - not simply from a literary or rhetorical viewpoint, but from the point of view of how actors might use this to guide their speaking of the lines, and to determine movement and action, reveals a three dimensional view of the characters and the nature of their relationship. Consider, for instance the line of verse which Caesar and Antony share when they first meet in *Antony and Cleopatra.*

Caesar:	*Welcome to Rome.*
Antony:	*Thank you.*
Caesar:	*Sit.*
Antony:	*Sit sir.*
Caesar:	*Nay, then.*

To the actors there are clear signals in the line, carried by the caesuras, that show this to be a power struggle between two strong, wilful men. The two last spondee feet in the line emphasise this. There is no civility implied in this verse lining with its caesura after almost every foot as students will discover as they explore the lines as actors. In exploring the play from this structural frame the students work primarily from theatre practitioner roles and use the range of strategies and techniques that are part of a rehearsal repertoire.

The third framing for the reading of the playscript is a semiotic frame. This frame focuses on the signals in the playscript that indicate how the ideas may have been represented on the stage for which Shakespeare wrote, and on how they might be transformed to another form or style of performance or space. The reader roles that best assist this way of reading the text are those of designer, director and dramaturge.

It is useful to conceptualise the signals in the text in terms of the notion of image. By image I mean the representation of ideas on stage. Images may be conceived of as being visual, dramatic, theatrical, auditory or verbal. While no image is exclusively the one or other, it assists the process of reading to schematise them thus.

Thus we might focus on the visual image of the crown, which Lear divides between Goneril and Regan, representing the idea of the kingdom about to be torn asunder. Or, we may consider the dramatic image contained in the action of Hal pushing Falstaff off the "throne" in *Henry IV Part 1* as an image of deposition. Theatrical images include those created by the action of the theatre technology, and in contemporary theatres would include such things as lighting fades, strobe lights, rear projections, smoke machines and so on. On Shakespeare's stage it would include such devices as onstage audience or play within the play. Students may be encouraged to explore the effect of the onstage audience in Lady Macbeth's sleepwalking scene as an image of the inevitability of discovery. Auditory images would also include those aspects of sound and music that communicate ideas, such as the musicians who play discordant music on the morning of the consummation of Othello's "marriage" to Desdemona. The verbal images, of course, include those key words in the dialogue that have echoes and resonances throughout the play.

In exploring the plays from this frame, students will use those activities appropriate to the assigned role – again drawing on all the rehearsal and production strategies that are normally part of the rehearsal and production process. This will include design sketches, blocking plans and other performance strategies as described in Michaels (1990).

Reading from this semiotic frame asks students to read the "words", conceptualise how those "words" might have been realised on a Shakespearian stage, conceptualise the images that an audience might have perceived, and transform those images into another form. I would argue that this is a complex and difficult form of abstract thinking – and yet that it is possible to have students achieve this through the type of workshop, experiential approaches that I have referred to throughout this chapter.

Although I have dealt with my three answers to the first of the outcomes questions I posed, I would also argue that the conditions of the second and third are contained in this way of satisfying the first. I believe that, through this active, practical, ensemble way of working, students will acquire the skills, and the values and attitudes as they come to terms with the knowledge and understanding.

In concluding, let me reiterate my central contention that Shakespeare's plays are significant, not so much because they represent the pinnacle of "our" cultural heritage – but rather, because they offer us the opportunity to know ourselves, our society and culture and our theatre.

(This chapter was originally presented by Wendy Michaels as a paper at the First International Conference for the Teaching of Shakespeare, Stratford-on-Avon, August 1992. It is reprinted here from THE NADIE Journal, Vol 17, No 2, 1993.)

Bibliography

Arnold, R (1987) "The Hidden Life of a Drama Text" in Corcoran,
    Bill and Evans, Emrys (eds), *Readers, Texts, Teachers*, New Jersey, Boynton Cook.

Aston, E & Savona G (1991) *Theatre as Sign System*, London, Routledge.

Boal, A (1992) translated by Adrian Jackson, *Games for Actors and Non-actors*, London, Routledge.

Bradley, A C (1904:1978) *Shakespearian Tragedy*, London, Macmillan.

Bartlett, B (1985) "Organisational Structure: The Key to Improved Comprehension and
    Recall" in Unsworth, Len (ed) (1985) *Reading an Australian Perspective*, Melbourne, Nelson.

Hayman, R (1977) *How to Read a Play*, London, Methuen.

Hughes, J (1992) "Enactment of the Expert: Drama and Reading Comprehension" in *The NADIE Journal*,
    Autumn 1992 vol 16 no 3.

Ingarden, R (1973) *The Literary Work of Art*, Evanstown, Northwestern University Press.

Meek, M (1988) *How Texts Teach What Readers Learn*, Great Britain, Thimble Press.

Michaels, Wendy & Newham, Peter (1987) *Inside Drama*, Melbourne, Pitman.

Michaels, Wendy (1990) *Played Upon A Stage*, Melbourne, Nelson.

Michaels, Wendy (1991) *The Theme of Honour's Tongue*, Sydney, St Clair Press.

Michaels, Wendy & Watson, K (1991) *The Dogs of War*, Sydney, St Clair Press.

Michaels, Wendy (1992) *Gaze On Cleopatra*, Sydney, St Clair Press.

Rosenblatt, L (1978) *The Reader, the Text, the Poem: the transactional theory
    of the literary work*, Carbondale, Southern Illinois University Press.

Styan, J L (1967) *Shakespeare's Stagecraft*, Cambridge University Press.

Unsworth, L (ed) (1985) *Reading: An Australian Perspective*, Melbourne, Nelson.

CHAPTER 2:
SHAKESPEARE'S THEATRE

Wendy Michaels

The Playhouse

The essential assumption upon which our approach to the study of any Shakespearian play is based is that the key to the unlocking of the layers of meaning rests with an examination of the form. In coming to terms with meaning in poetry it is necessary to take into account the form or genre. Similarly in the novel, or other prose forms, the narrative structure must be considered in determining meanings. This is no less true of the drama. Meaning and form in the drama cannot be separated. We do need to consider the whole physical reality of the theatre for which each play has been written. This includes such aspects as the size and shape of the acting space, the architecture of the auditorium and the availability of technical apparatus, costuming, lighting and other special effects.

In a playhouse where the convention of sophisticated lighting exists, much meaning can be communicated visually. Similarly a theatre with the facilities for elaborate sets allows for visual communication of meanings without recourse to weighty words. And, moreover, in a theatre where it is customary for the audience to sit in darkened silence during a play it is unnecessary for a playwright to employ catalogues of metaphors to make a single point.

Needless to say, none of this was available to Shakespeare as he wrote his plays for performance at The Globe.

For a variety of reasons, not least of which is historical distance, we do not have easy access to detailed and accurate information on all aspects of the Elizabethan theatre scene. The available information presents us with a complexly interwoven tapestry of confusing and sometimes conflicting data from which it is, nevertheless, possible to tease out sufficient threads to assist us in our reconstructions.

Despite distinctions drawn between the public and private theatres of the time, basically what we have in the Elizabethan theatre is a development from the situation of the medieval inn yard performances where the audience all but completely surrounded the players, who were performing from a raised platform. The close proximity between actor and audience encouraged an interactive theatre where improvisation was possible and indeed acceptable. The Elizabethan theatres clustered on the south bank of the Thames in order to be outside the jurisdiction of officialdom – a factor which hints at bawdy or risque elements within the performances. Essentially the theatre was a round wooden building with an external diameter of approximately 80 feet. The walls held perhaps three galleries with seating space. There was apparently no seating in the pit of the auditorium. Thrusting into the central part of the auditorium was a platform stage of immense proportions – 40 feet wide and nearly 30 feet deep. The back of the acting space was a permanent architectural structure without facilities for a changing cyclorama of scenery flats. Two doors on either side of this structure provided the primary entrances and exits for the stage.

The auditorium was capable of accommodating 2,000 people – approximately 400 more than the Opera Theatre at the Sydney Opera House – and yet the enclosing shape meant that no member of the audience need be more than 50 feet from the stage.

The physical reality of this theatre shape and size determined to a large extent the style of play to be performed there. The fixed stage backdrop with no possibility of actual scenic changes demanded not only that the playwright set the scene in words, but also that costumes and props had to work to indicate aspects of change, and that alterations of mood had to be achieved through tone and pace of language, and through music. But it also precluded a naturalistic form of play. There was no pretence that the audience were watching anything other than a "play"! The fourth wall was not yet in existence. Thus characters could be accepted as non-naturalistic, and witches and ghosts were not out of place.

Not only are we able to view characters in a different way, but time and place have different perspectives within a non-naturalistic framework. It is undoubtedly significant that the addition of scene setting captions was made after the Restoration and for a stage of vastly different characteristics.

The close proximity between players and audience allowed a style of theatre performance and play structure that is not possible in other theatres, as for instance a proscenium arch stage. Asides and soliloquy, for instance, are a feature of such a stage and theatre shape. These devices are a direct address to the acknowledged audience. There is no fourth wall between player and audience and it is therefore possible, acceptable and indeed desirable that there be communication between the two. It may well be that this communication was in fact a two way activity with audience actively commenting on the action on stage to the players themselves.

The lack of changing visual imagery on the large open bare stage might appear to be a constraint for the playwright. But this is not so. What it means is that the emphasis has been shifted from the visual to the verbal and dramatic imagery, and the visual imagery of the costumes and the few props that do appear.

Costumes become an important way of signalling change. This may be an important aspect of the play's structure. Three changes of costume are common, particularly for a tragic hero. Consider the significance of Lear's change from Royal robes to the shedding of all his vestments in the storm to the donning of a nightshirt. This provides a visual metaphor for the journey he makes during the play.

The facility of costume changes also allows for plays based around the issues of disguise. It is easy to dismiss these plays as an excuse to allow male actors playing female roles to revert to male clothing on stage for the bulk of the play. This, however is altogether too glib and ethnocentric an explanation, and certainly does not hold true when applied to a play such as *The Merchant of Venice* where the actors playing Portia and Nerissa are only in disguise as males for the fourth act. What is more important is to view the character disguise as part of the theatrical convention of role doubling. Seeing Portia as the Doctor in the court scene enhances our view of Portia in terms of her domestic situation.

The lack of fixed scenery and scene changes also affects the tempo of the play. Coupled with the fact that the plays were performed in daylight on fine days with the audience also in the light, there was no need for artificial scene breaks. The play moved from one scene to the next fluidly. This meant that the playwright had to look to the rhythmic pattern which he wanted to establish to manipulate mood. Thus the order of scenes is determined not by the plot but by the atmosphere which they will create.

The size and shape of the stage enhances this effect. It is a very large space which invites movement and the grouping and regrouping of actors in a variety of configurations. It allows scenes of grand processionals, balls, fights, chases, crowds, orators, eavesdropping, intimate love scenes, death scenes, suicides, murders and the very successful play-within-the-play. All the scenes follow one another in a fluid way without the break or pause that we have grown accustomed to in modern theatre where curtains fall, lights are dimmed, and bar sales at interval are an important part of the theatre's financial statement.

Just as this theatre did not rely on the services of a scenic designer, neither did it rely on a director. Essentially it was an actor's and playwright's theatre. Thus directions to the actor needed to be contained within the fabric of the text. The ubiquitous line - "See, where he comes" - is in fact a stage direction indicating an entrance of a character who has just been discussed. This also signals to the audience the identity of the characters in the play - there being no "programs" for purchase in the foyer prior to the show. The rhyming couplet is another common stage direction - this time signalling the exit of a character or characters. Other directions for business such as kneeling, kissing, fighting and so on are incorporated within the speech of the characters.

The variety of scenes enables the actor to exploit his talents to the full. The playwright's reliance on the actor's voice, gesture and movement encouraged him to write a drama rich in vocal variation. There is the obvious difference between the verse and prose passages - the latter not merely included for the groundlings - but within each there are carefully crafted shifts of tone, rhythm, pace and pitch.

Much has been written about Shakespeare's sources. Original versions of his stories are located by scholars in order to show the derivative nature of his plots. Indeed no one would dispute that Shakespeare was something of an arch-plagiarist, and it was quite probable that his plots, his stories were well known to his audiences. However, the Elizabethan audience were obviously unperturbed by this. It would appear that they did not necessarily go to see "what will happen next". That is essentially a modern idea derived perhaps from radio or cinema serials. The Elizabethan audience went to see what the playwright and actor did with a story known to them. This, added to the intimacy of the audience/actor relationship and the lightened auditorium presupposes differing audience conventions to those to which we have grown accustomed. We cannot assume that the audience stood or sat silently in their places. Instead, it is much more likely that they were mobile and vocal. This has implications for the patterns of movement and grouping on the stage. There is no such thing on a thrust stage as having "your back to the audience". There would inevitably be audience behind some actors at times. While backs can be expressive, they do have a tendency to obliterate or distort the sounds of the speech. Thus it's obvious that mobility on the stage is to be a crucial aspect of the acting style.

Where groups are to be static for any length of time careful placement is necessary. Downstage areas, by their proximity to the audience, become key areas for intimate scenes and particularly for scenes of action. Upstage areas are more distanced and therefore suitable for the more static, ceremonial or eavesdropping scenes.

The thrust stage also provides very strong diagonal lines to suggest conflict and opposition. This is further reinforced by the presence of two doors, which may take on an almost symbolic significance in a play such as *Romeo and Juliet*.

Much has been made of the balcony and obviously in a play such as *Romeo and Juliet* it is an essential ingredient of the enactment of the lovers' story. However it is not essential to all Shakespeare's plays and it has been given undue prominence at the expense of more important conventions. The same is true of the trapdoor that is undoubtedly used in *Hamlet*.

An aspect that has also been given undue prominence is the supposed inner stage. This device has been credited with enabling eavesdropping scenes, the setting of scenes and drawing back of curtains and other such facilities. Styan doubts that the inner stage was a regular convention of the Elizabethan stage, and asserts that intimate scenes would not be played so far upstage, and moreover that the setting of a scene behind a curtain would have destroyed the symphonic pattern of the play.

Shakespeare's Audience

Theatre does not exist without an audience. Shakespeare's audiences were frequent attenders, and many had travelled far to view the plays as evidenced in the comments of Thomas Platter, a German traveller who attended a performance at The Curtain in 1959. He wrote, inter alia,

"... at two in the afternoon, London has two, sometimes three plays running in different places, competing with each other, and those which play best obtain most spectators."

At the time that Shakespeare wrote London had a population of approximately 150,000. Estimates of audience attendance figures suggest that about 15,000 people per week attended plays - a figure of around 10% of the population.

Differential entry prices obtained, with groundlings paying less than those who sought seats in the galleries. It is often assumed that the groundlings lacked the understanding of the finer points of the plays, and were generally looking only to be entertained by the low life characters in the plays. However it seems unlikely from the available evidence that this view represents anything other than the snobbery of later generations' perceptions. What is more likely is that the public playhouses appealed to a mass audience with all members appreciating various aspects of the play. Indeed it would appear that the theatre was something of a leveller, as indicated in the epigram of John Davies:

> For as we see at all the playhouse doors
> When ended is the play, the dance, the song,
> A thousand townsmen, gentlemen, and whores,
> Porters and serving men together throng ...

The audience, up to two thousand at a time in the public playhouses, did not sit in silence. They were able to buy food and drink, move about, talk with other audience members, and interact with the players. Perhaps what caused some interjections between members of the audience were the hats which all Elizabethans wore indoors as well as out. The higher the hat, the higher the status of the wearer – and this must surely have occasioned comment as a hat obscured the view of another audience member.

Another feature much remarked upon was the presence of the obtrusive smells. There were smells of the artisans' occupations, of garlic – a recent addition to the diet – of tobacco brought from Virginia, and of urine, *giving out a pleasant odour*, as Platter noted.

The audiences of the Elizabethan playhouse were viewed by the Puritans as riotous and immoral. There certainly is some evidence of violence and lawlessness, and no doubt pickpockets and prostitutes plied their trade throughout the audience. However Busino, a Venetian, describes the scene at The Fortune in 1617 rather differently:

"... a crowd of nobility, so very well arrayed that they looked like so many princes, listening as silently and soberly as possible. These theatres are frequented by a number of respectable and handsome ladies ..."

From the players' point of view the most common complaint about the audience had to do with the noise of hazelnuts being cracked, and later from those members of the audience who took to placing themselves on stools on the stage – a practice that began in the indoor theatres and later spread to the open air theatres. The Globe, however, did not permit stools on its stage.

As Andrew Gurr points out, "A crowd always has a collective personality of its own, and its mood, whether laughing or crying or objecting to what is happening on stage is infectious. Today we usually receive Shakespeare, or indeed any play, in respectful and sometimes bored silence. Elizabethans were more active in their reactions ..."

Shakespeare's Actors

Players companies in Shakespeare's day were co-operative, collaborative ventures. Generally they comprised about seven or eight men who played all parts with some judicious doubling of roles. The parts of women were taken by young boy apprentices, and any parts left over were taken by the hired men – the equivalent of extras today. Like the prompt or bookholder these men were paid a wage. The other members of the company were 'sharers' and held a share in the company. The company resources comprised the material assets of the play, books and the costumes, and the immaterial assets of the collective skills of the company members.

Within the companies, particular names stood out as the stars of the company, and these people were hailed by audiences for their skills as actors. Richard Burbage and William Kempe were two of the foremost stars. Burbage was the first actor to play Hamlet, Othello, Lear, Antony, Coriolanus and Richard III, and he played most of the leading parts in Shakespeare's plays. Kempe was the company clown who was renowned for his role as Falstaff.

Shakespeare belonged to the company known as the Lord Chamberlain's Men until the death of Queen Elizabeth and thereafter as the King's Men. In this company he wrote plays, acted and managed the company. Although the company was forced to travel from London at times it holds the record for the longest running company – forty-eight years.

In the city the companies operated a repertory system that allowed about three weeks of rehearsal for a new play. There was a rapid turnover of plays that saw actors rehearsing each morning and performing each afternoon with Sundays off. Each day saw a different play performed. Travelling in the country saw different conditions with few plays, and few costumes and props.

Parts in plays tended to be cast on the basis of type – a necessity given the basis of their working conditions. It is assumed that Shakespeare even wrote particular parts for particular actors. Each player received only his part of the play – his own lines and the cue lines. Only the bookholder had the full script, and was able to put up in the tiring house the complete plot, and the patterns of entrances and exits.

Players were also expected to be skilled in some aspects of music. Most of Shakespeare's plays involve some music, song or dance, and oftentimes this involved a player accompanying himself on the lute or some other instrument. William Kempe, for instance, had a reputation for his dancing skills immortalised in his Morris Dance known as the *Nine Days' Wonder*. Kempe's comic and improvisational skills are thought to be the butt of Hamlet's remarks about clowns who speak more than is set down for them.

Players were also expected to be able to acquit themselves with the sword, and it seems from the number of single sword duels in the plays that in fact they were able to do so with some degree of expertise.

The boy actors apprenticed to the adult companies were bound for several years, usually entering the company around the age of ten, and playing female parts until the voice broke, usually by the age of nineteen.

Acting in plays was a customary part of the education of youth in schools in the sixteenth century. Brinsley wrote in his *Ludus Literarius* of the values of playing in the education of children. The adult companies certainly sought the best talent in the declamatory arts of rhetoric, pronunciation and gesture.

Versatility and the ability to move the audience to tears was greatly prized: *Not only by their speaking but by their acting they drew tears ...*

Acting Styles

In Shakespeare's time the term acting meant the art of gesture. It referred to the actions of the orator. Bulwer's publication in 1644 of *Chirologia, or the Natural Language of the Hand* demonstrates the positions of the hand in relation to the rest of the body to indicate particular gestures that are appropriate to particular emotions.

Acting was distinguished from the term "playing", which initially was used pejoratively to describe the players of The Kings' Servants. Playing seemed to imply a lack of skill in communicating the appropriate gesture for the emotion.

By 1600 the term "personation" had been coined. This term encompassed the notion that the actor would "qualify everything according to the nature of the person personated". Personation seemed to mark a change in direction in acting style from the broad extemporising generalisations to a more particularisation of character.

The coining of this term coincided with the demise of the comic extemporising clowns and the rise of the great tragedians such as Alleyn and Burbage. The pantomimic actions which derived from commedia dell'arte were gradually being replaced by a differing style of acting. This also occurred as the private, indoor theatres were producing seasons of plays alongside the public outdoor arena theatres.

Many of Shakespeare's plays make reference to styles of acting or performance. Hamlet gives advice to the actors who are to perform the play - "Suit the action to the word, the word to the action" with his special observance, that "you o'erstep not the modesty of nature ..." the purpose of playing is ..."to hold the mirror up to nature." It is possible today to distinguish three broad acting styles:
1. oratorical or declamatory
2. method or naturalistic
3. gestic or representational.

Oratorical or declamatory acting is usually associated with non-naturalistic drama, poetic monologue, stereotypical characters, unrealistic or fantastical scenarios, and large auditoria, where big gestures and ringing tones are needed to reach the whole audience. Oratorical acting tends to be concerned with the visual exterior of the character stereotype.

This is the style of acting that we associate with Bottom's performance of Pyramus, and probably is the type of acting that Kempe used in his extemporising comic roles. It is certainly the style of acting that Hamlet is criticising.

Gestic or representational acting is concerned with the representation of a character through actions and reactions. It is usually associated with non-naturalistic theatre, often involving dialogue, monologue, music and song, as well as direct address to the audience. It is usually associated with smaller acting spaces, and often concerned with the more tragic themes. Although this style of acting was essentially described by Brecht, it would seem to be very close to the style of acting referred to as "personation" in Shakespeare's time.

Method or naturalistic acting is generally associated with realistic plays, film, and TV. It is usually concerned with realistic characters in real settings and situations, speaking real dialogue, where the audience is unacknowledged either because of the fourth wall or the TV or cinema screen. Method acting is concerned with the inner life of the characters, their motivations and psyches. It is closely linked with the psychological interpretation of characters in literature, and with the work of Stanislavsky, and plays such as those of Ibsen or Chekhov.

From the late nineteenth century method acting processes have been applied to the plays of Shakespeare, and this has produced some readings and performances that may differ from those of the original players.

CHAPTER 3: GETTING USED TO THE LANGUAGE

Wendy Michaels

The language of the plays does not have to be a barrier to students' reading and performing of the plays. There is no need to translate the text into modern English. What is required is that students translate the text into action. But students do need to know that the language of Shakespeare's England was the precursor to our modern English. They need to understand that it is essentially the same language, but that language being a living thing is subject to change. One potential source of difficulty is the presence in the text of particular words with which the students may not be familiar. Words such as "murrion", "forsooth", and "sirrah" are unlikely to have been encountered by students as they are now obsolete. Other words such as "fond", "presently" and "counsels" have changed their meanings with the passage of time. To assist with this problem most editions used in schools have explanatory footnotes. It is sufficient to direct students to these footnotes as an **aid** to their understanding of the text. But it is essential that they use them only as required - for overdependence on the footnotes breaks up the flow of the text and ultimately impedes understanding of the play as a whole.

Another source of potential difficulty may be the verb endings and auxiliaries, such as "hath" and "doth", and the pronouns such as "thee" and "thou". It is a simple matter to relate these forms to their contemporary equivalents - not in a form that has to be learned by heart, but merely as a point of interest. Students may wish to try out these forms in improvisations.

The frequency of the apostrophe of omission is another source of potential difficulty that can be readily allayed. The rhythm of the lines is very important and Shakespeare has employed the apostrophe to enhance the rhythmic patterns. Students need to be made aware of the patterns and how the use of the apostrophe serves this end. Students might experiment with filling in the gaps and noting the altered rhythmic pattern.

Within each play the form shifts from prose to blank verse. This was not a device to enable the groundlings to comprehend the action, or for comic relief, or even to distinguish the noble characters from the plebs. Prince Hal speaks prose in *Henry IV Part I* and Macbeth writes in prose to his wife. The changes are much more concerned with the rhythm and mood of the play. A thrust stage invites movement and allows for varieties of rhythmic patterns. The plays exploit this through the language patterns which suggest movement and rhythm and pace.

Important, too, is the use of music and song, which was seen as an integral part of the performance, and not merely as "background" as we tend to view it today.

The *Shakespeare Workshop Series* gives considerable attention to ways of helping students to become accustomed to Shakespeare's language. Most of the booklets offer two or three units in which the possibilities of rhythm and tense can be explored before study of the play is begun. See also, in the chapter 'A Range of Activities', the following: alter ego, cloze, group soliloquy, kaleidoscope, sequencing.

Speaking the Verse

The iambic metrical foot has two beats in it - a short beat followed by a long beat. There are usually five of these feet in each line of Shakespeare's verse. He does however vary this pattern to indicate to the players changes of rhythm and pace in their delivery and in their movements.

Caesura

Each line of blank verse may contain a caesura or cut in the line, that is often indicted by punctuation such as the comma, semi-colon, dash, question mark or full stop. These punctuation markers did not indicate a pause to the actors, but rather the importance of moving on to the end of the line.

Students should be invited to explore such lines, first of all pausing at the caesura, and then reading the whole line without a pause to hear the differences in meaning that are expressed.

The caesura allows the actor to take a quick breath before proceeding to the end of the line, or, in the case of an enjambed line, running on to the next line.

Enjambment

Where the sense of the blank verse runs on to the next line without any punctuation markers at the end of the line, the player should use a suspensive pause. This allows the slightest elongation of the last syllable of the line before proceeding to the next line, so that there is the impression of continuation but the rhythmical pattern is not lost.

Verse Lining

Verse lining involves two or more characters sharing a single line of verse. The punctuation at the end of the first speaker's line acts as a caesura, and the second character is interrupting the first in order to keep the flow of the rhythm of the iambic pentameter.

Edmund Kean as Richard III

CHAPTER 4:
A RANGE OF ACTIVITIES

Wendy Michaels and Ken Watson

(See also 'Glossary')

Abbreviations

In this book the following abbreviations refer to volumes in the *Shakespeare Workshop Series*:

AC	*Gaze on Cleopatra: Antony and Cleopatra*
AYL	*Love's Keen Arrows: As You Like It*
HAM	*A Workshop Approach to Hamlet*
HIV	*The Theme of Honour's Tongue: Henry IV, Part I*
HV	*We Happy Few: Henry V*
JC	*The Dogs Of War: Julius Caesar*
KL	*Sharper Than A Serpent's Tooth: King Lear*
MA	*A Skirmish Of Wit: Much Ado About Nothing*
MAC	*Creative Work Ideas for Macbeth*
MM	*Some by Virtue Fall: Measure for Measure*
MND	*The Course of True Love: A Midsummer Night's Dream*
MSS	*A Dagger of the Mind: Macbeth for Senior Students*
MV	*Let Him Look to His Bond: The Merchant of Venice*
MWW	*Moonshine Revellers: The Merry Wives of Windsor*
OTH	*The Green-Ey'd Monster: Othello*
RIII	*To Prove A Villain: Richard III*
RJ	*Star-Cross'd Lovers: Romeo and Juliet*
RWT	*Bitter Bread: Richard II* and *The Winter's Tale*
TEM	*Full Fathom Five: The Tempest*
TN	*The Food of Love: Twelfth Night*
TS	*Such a Mad Marriage: The Taming of the Shrew*

Alter Ego

This is a useful device for exploring the subtext (qv, Glossary). It is spelt out in detail in **TN** (Activity 10), and can be used when exploring most plays. The students, in groups of four, take an important stretch of dialogue involving two characters. They then prepare a script in which, after each character has spoken, his/her alter ego says what the character is really thinking. The activity requires a close attention to the lines, and can also be very amusing, since the alter ego is usually scripted to speak in modern colloquial English.

In **MV** (Activity 11), Greg Seach offers a variation on this activity which he calls "interior duologue". The students work in pairs. One says the lines (usually of a long speech) while the other says aloud the thoughts and feelings of the character. See also **MSS** (Activity 8).

Auditions (see Interviews)

Bare Bones

This activity involves getting the students, in groups, to work on a given scene or section of a scene to reduce the piece to its bare bones, preserving the most important lines and actions, and preparing a script for performance to the class. See **HAM** (Activity 17).

Blocking

Before rehearsals begin, a director normally prepares a set of blocking plans on which he/she has plotted the basic stage movements (see figure 1). The advantage of this method for students is that they become aware of the realities of the stage space and its own theatrical peculiarities, and for the thrust stage this means they come to terms with the fluidity of movement across the stage and the restrictions of the two doors in terms of entrances and exits.

There are a number of ways of using this technique. Using a basic plan of the thrust stage on a whiteboard or photocopied on sheets of paper, or on overhead transparencies, students working in groups can be allocated units or scenes for which they must draw up a director's plan. They need to decide on symbols for characters, and note the points in the text when major changes

FIGURE 1

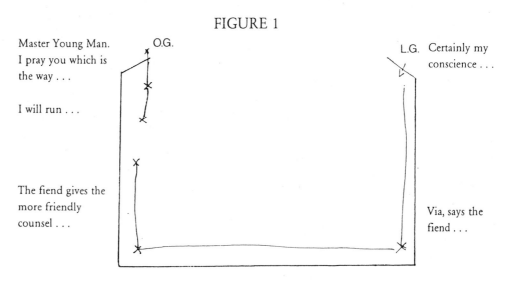

Master Young Man.
I pray you which is
the way . . .

O.G.

L.G. Certainly my
conscience . . .

I will run . . .

The fiend gives the
more friendly
counsel . . .

Via, says the
fiend . . .

The Merchant of Venice
Act II scene ii, lines 1-35 - Blocking Plan

occur. From this exercise students begin to realise the way the stage invites movement patterns, and sets up shapes on the stage which heighten tension.

After each group has drawn up their blocking plans it should be possible to test out each plan and to see how it works. The actual size of the stage should be borne in mind. Students could then be encouraged to modify plans which do not work well, to recreate other plans, or to cut lines from the text which would make their plans work within the space. This is, after all, exactly what a director has to be prepared to do, and in order to do it effectively it is necessary to know the text well, and to understand the space. Thus the students are sent continually back to justify the decisions they have made.

A further extension of this activity could be to change the shape of the stage – say to a proscenium arch, or theatre in the round – and ask students to examine the changes necessary for a performance in this shape.

Follow-up writing activities for this exercise are various. Students could be asked in the role of director to write a report to the board of directors outlining the plan for a proposed production, or a memo to the stage manager outlining requirements for the production, and noting any expected difficulties, or an outline of a speech to be given to the cast at the first rehearsal. Alternatively students could be asked to assume roles as actors and to write journals, letters etc, discussing the way the director has blocked the play. There are, too, a variety of traditional essay type written activities that could focus on a particular scene, and discussion of the action and mood of the scene.

Many of the volumes in the Shakespeare Workshop Series contain blocking activities. **HV** (Activity 16), **MV** (Activity 6), **OTH** (Activity 4), **RIII** (Activity 22), **TN** (Activity 12), **TS** (Activity 11), **MND** (Activities 6, 10) contain detailed instructions for a blocking activity using the shape and measurements of Shakespeare's stage.

Bystanders

Often in key scenes in Shakespeare there are characters present who do not speak. Students, in groups, can prepare additional scenes in which these characters comment on what they have witnessed (the basis of Tom Stoppard's *Rosencrantz and Guildenstern Are Dead*). See, for example, **HAM** (Activity 12), **KL** (Activity 14), **MV** (Activity 14), **MSS** (Activity 9).

Character Profiles and Spider Charts

Where a play is being prepared for an examination, students (in pairs) can be asked to build up 'character profiles' using key lines from the particular character's speeches, as well as words, phrases, pictures or photographs that depict that character. The profiles are displayed as wall posters, **HIV** (Activity 4), **MSS** (Activity 19). Another good revision activity is to prepare a "This Is Your Life" program for a key character (see **HIV** Activity 14, **MV** Activity 13, sheet 2).

A spider chart is a way of helping students make up their minds about complex characters. In the centre of a large sheet of paper, write the name of the protagonist (or other major character) and around that name at a distance, place the names of other major characters. Arrows are shown pointing from the protagonist to each of the others, and students are asked to write a short quotation along each arrow to sum up what they decide is the protagonist's view of each character. On a second chart, which reverses the direction of the arrows, students place quotations to indicate the feelings of each of the characters about the protagonist. **TEM** (Activity 4, **RWT** (Activity 5).

Charting Relationships

Where a play has a large number of characters, it sometimes helps to have pupils prepare charts which show the links among the characters. A charting activity focussing on Prospero's relationships with the other character in the play is to be found in **TEM** (Activity 4). Students construct a spider chart with Prospero's name in the centre, and arrows leading to the names of other characters with whom he is closely involved. Then they write along each arrow a quotation indicating Prospero's feelings towards that character. A second chart, reversing the arrows, could be used to indicate the feelings of the other characters about Prospero. See also **HAM** (Activity 19), **MV** (Activity 9), **MSS** (Activity 14), **RIII** (Activity 4).

An allied activity is the production of **stress graphs** (like those seen on the machines that monitor the condition of patients in intensive care) for important characters. A stress graph for Macbeth, for example, would show high points at the killing of Duncan and the appearance of Banquo's ghost.

Cloze (see also Jigsaw Cloze)

A good activity for helping students become familiar with Shakespeare's language. Before the reading/acting of the play has begun, the students, in groups of three or four, are presented with a speech in which six or seven key words have been deleted. They are asked to decide on appropriate words to fill the blanks. The task requires them to use not only the sematic cues, but the metrical cues as well. See, for example, **TN** (Activity 9), **HAM** (Activity 5), **MND** (Activity 17), **OTH** (Activity 3), **RJ** (Activity 2), **TS** (Activity 3).

Coat of Arms

Designing a coat of arms for an important character (or family) can be a challenging activity. See **TN** (Activity 7).

Collage

The word 'collage' comes from a French term meaning 'sticking/pasting things on'. In art, then, it denotes a work that contains a mixture of media; in literature it refers to works containing a mixture of allusions, quotations, references, foreign expressions. The collage activity suggested here combines the two forms: groups construct posters which may display pictures, quotations, highlighted words etc. It is a particularly useful way of giving visual shape to the thematic concerns of a play, **MND** (Activity 21), **TN** (Activity 8), **TS** (Activity 12).

Performed Collage

Performed collages use the same principle as visual collage. They involve the selection of images, segments of scenes from previously scripted drama, or from improvised drama.

In working with Shakespeare's texts this may involve students in the selection of lines, segments or scenes from a particular character, a particular point of view, a particular set of images and so on. For instance, the collage may focus on women in Shakespeare's plays, or on a character such as Hamlet, or Henry IV, or Falstaff or Brutus.

In selecting images, lines, moments etc, it is important that student consider the sequencing of the items selected, and ways of linking items. Links may be achieved through the use of freeze, or through music, blackout, dissolve, slow motion sculptures and so on.

Costume Design

Students could be asked to design costumes for the characters. They would need to decide on the period in which the play is set, and then decide whether they are aiming for authenticity or adaptation. Once an overall design concept has been decided upon individual students could be allotted a particular character to research through the text, to establish the actions which this character must perform, the general features of the character and any props which this character must use. Each student could then design costume and props for the character. This could be done with sketches, or by using photographs, photocopies, etc.

See **HV** (Activity 18), **JC** (Activity 11), **MAC** (Activity 4), **TN** (Activity 17), **TS** (Activity 5), **MM** (Activity 17). See also Part B: A Shakespeare Festival.

Cut Versions

Throughout their stage history most of Shakespeare's plays have been cut, rewritten or otherwise changed. Indeed, even the productions most faithful to the text make cuts (eg: rarely is the clown scene in *Othello* included in modern productions) and film versions of necessity shorten the plays radically. Activities which focus on producing shortened versions can be quite useful.

See for example, **HIV** (Activity 13), **KL** (Activity 12), **MA** (Activity 12), **OTH** (Activity 8), **RJ** (Activities 13, 20), **TN** (Activity 11). In **HAM** (Activity 11), students are invited to examine some of the changes that Betterton and Garrick made to the text of *Hamlet*.

Diary, Speaking (see Tableau)

Dreams

In *A Workshop Approach to Hamlet*, Brenda Pinder suggests that a group take a "crisis point" for a character and then devise a dream he or she might have had at that point. See also **MSS** (Activity 18) which asks students to use the model of the dream in *Richard III* as a model for Macbeth's dream.

Dumbshow

In *Hamlet*, a "dumbshow" gives the outline of "The Mousetrap", the play-within-the-play. This technique can be used to highlight the main elements of any play being studied. See, for example, **KL** (Activity 17), **OTH** (Activity 17), **HAM** (Activity 14), **MSS** (Activity 17).

Film Review

See **HV** (Activity 19).

Film Script (see also Storyboarding)

As a prelude to viewing and discussing a film or video of a Shakespearian play, a good activity is to have students prepare a film script of a key scene. Instructions for this activity can be found in **RJ** (Activity 15). See also **TEM** (Activity 8).

Freeze Frames

Frames are rather like shop windows at Christmas time. Through a series of static pictures they tell a story. The focus here is not only on the body language of the individual characters but also on the relationships between the characters and the ways these are expressed through space.

As with sculpting this technique is adaptable. It can be used with the teacher as omniscient narrator recounting the play's action in sequence. The students are divided into groups to set up the frames for the action sequence. This needs to be well prepared. The teacher needs to know how many characters are needed for each sequence and to allocate groups accordingly. As it may happen that there will be different students in each sequence representing the same character some other visual aids to indicate character identity may be needed. This could be a representative prop or item of clothing that is passed quickly from frame to frame. Alternatively characters could wear name tags. Each group may need four or five frames for its sequence depending on the complexity of the action. Arrange the groups in order so that there is as little delay as possible between each sequence.

While each group sets up the frame, the other students keep their eyes closed so that they experience a shutter effect thus:

Eyes closed	frame 1 setting up
Eyes open	frame 1 held 15-20 seconds
Eyes closed	frame 2 setting up
Eyes open	frame 2 held 15-20 seconds

and so on.

This is one of the most effective techniques for establishing dramatic action and reinforcing the structure of the play. It highlights for students the ways in which layers of meaning are derived from a patterning of scene sequences rather than a linear plot line. The cinematic effect of this activity mirrors the effect of the play on the large stage.

Frames can be further adapted so that the class work from the script itself to produce the frames. This again requires careful planning and preparation on the part of the teacher. A whole long scene, or a series of shorter scenes would provide the basis for this activity. The scene or scenes need to be divided into manageable units. These may only be a few lines, or several lines depending on the density of the text at this point. Groups are divided and allocated according to the number of characters required for each unit.

Each group, having been allocated its unit, must make a close reading of the script to determine how many frames they require, and to explore the signals to the actor, as well as any subtextual aspects. The groups are given time to do this and to set up the requisite frames. Again character name tags, or representational costume items or props may assist in character identification.

The use of frames in this fashion can be further extended. Each group is asked to find a key line for each character within each frame. This demands a careful reading and deciding of the dramatic focal point for each character. The frames are then run through again, but for each frame, although the positions are frozen, each character utters in sequence the key line.

This is really an adaptation of the "instant book" technique. But importantly the instant play has grown out of the visual and dramatic as well as the verbal.

A camera is a useful tool to capture these explorations and the resultant photographs can be used in conjunction with the key lines as captions to make a "picture book" of the play. The question could be raised as to whether a narrator is needed, and this may well lead back to the text to see how Shakespeare fills in relevant background information through the narrative recounted by particular characters.

See **HAM** (Activity 7), **HV** (Activity 15), **MAA** (Activity 9), **MND** (Activity 15), **TEM** (Activities 5, 31), **TN** (Activity 18), **MSS** (Activity 17), **RIII** (Activity 10).

Games

Michael Hayhoe (**MAC** Activity 1) has developed a card game for *Macbeth* designed to help students review the text collaboratively. It can easily be adapted for use with other plays. The Q & A game in **TEM** (Activity 18) can also be adapted for other plays. Oxford Games Ltd (UK) has produced a board game, *Playing Shakespeare*, originally designed for adults but usable from year 8 upwards.

Another game from *Creative Work Ideas for Macbeth* that can be adapted for use with other plays is "Guess Who?" (Activity 5), a game which encourages students to make complex judgements about characters.

In *Shakespeare in the Classroom* (Open University Press) Susan Leach outlines a casket game as an introduction to *The Merchant of Venice* (pp115-6).

Group Soliloquy

Group soliloquy is a good way of getting students accustomed to the language of a play. Choose a soliloquy that will divide into sense units of roughly the same number as there are students in the class. Allocate one sense unit to each. After each has had a chance to try out his/her piece in a few different ways, arrange the class in a circle (in the correct order) and have them read the speech through. By the second time through, the feeling behind the words should become evident. See **HAM** (Activity 9), **KL** (Activity 18), **MND** (Activity 3), **TEM** (Activity 13), **TN** (Activity 2), **MSS** (Activity 12), **RIII** (Activity 5).

Brenda Pinder (**KL** Activity 18) suggests that this activity can be taken a step further by performing the speech - with movement as it suggests itself - to theatrical effect. Students can speak from the edges of the room and move in to form a group at the centre, or move around addressing the lines to others in the circle. As the students become more involved, they will start making suggestions about how the performance can be improved.

Hot Seat

This activity involves a member of the class stepping into the role of a character, speaking as that character and answering the audience's questions (and the questions of other characters). It is particularly useful as a revision activity. See **HAM** (Activity 20), **MAA** (Activity 20), **TEM** (Activity 20), **TN** (Activity 19), **MSS** (Activity 16), **RIII** (Activity 17), **MWW** (Activity 18).

Imaginative Recreation

The real value of writing in what has been called the mode of imaginative recreation lies in the demands such writing makes on the students' independent personal response to the text, detailed knowledge and understanding of the script, language facility and imagination. It is impossible in this type of writing to regurgitate the views of critics, peers, teachers or cribs. The form demands an individual response, closely in line with syllabus objectives. But just as it is demanding of the student, so is it of the teacher. It is vital that the tasks set be realistic in terms of the context of the play.

One needs to assess carefully the value of a question which asks a student in the role of Hamlet to discuss his mother fixation with a psychiatrist as opposed to one which asks a student in the role of Jessica to write the letter to Lorenzo which has occasioned her elopement with him. Where situations that are essentially outside the text are to be used, it is important that they do demand that the student understand the complexity of the character, make some sort of moral judgement about him or her, and use as much of the textual material as possible.

The confession is one way of doing this. Macbeth, for instance, may be seeking entry to heaven and may be required to explain to St Peter his actions on earth. Counsel for the defence is another way of structuring a confession situation. This time, however, it could be written as a duologue with the character explaining the situation to his solicitor and the solicitor posing questions or seeking to clarify motivations. This could even be expanded to a script for the court case.

Imaginative recreation exercises pose something of a problem with Shakespearian plays because of their non-naturalistic nature. However, there are a number of points within the play where a situation can be extended along the lines of the "missing scene" exercise (q.v.). Portia's last lines of the play, for instance ...

> ... Let us go in
> and charge us there upon inter'gatories
> And we will answer all things faithfully.

could be the basis of such a task, students being asked to write the offstage scene in which Portia explains all, or to recount the scene in narrative form.

MAC (Activity 10), **TEM** (Activity 1, sheet 2), **MSS** (Activity 10).

Improvisation
(Including Role Play)

This is a valuable tool to use in exploring the subtleties of subtextual meaning, and is also a way of opening up the issues before a play is begun.

There are four different types of improvisation which can prove useful in exploring Shakespearian texts within the context of the classroom.

1. Parallel Improvisation
2. Improvisation Based on Characters
3. Improvisation Based on Lines
4. Improvisation Set Within the Text

Parallel Improvisation

In a parallel improvisation the situation or conflict is parallel with one in the text but the context is altered. There are many ways of setting up parallel improvisations. A series of conflicts extracted from the play and reset in other contexts could be allocated to various groups within the class. Thus the opening scene of *A Midsummer Night's Dream* could be explored through these parallel improvisations:

⚙ Two lovers talk of their coming marriage.

⚙ A Greek father drags his daughter before the priest because she is refusing to marry the man of his choice and wants instead to marry an Australian.

⚙ The young Australian man is also summoned before the priest.

⚙ The Australian and the Greek girl meet secretly and decide to elope.

⚙ The Greek girl tells her best friend of her plans.

In each case the outcome of the improvisation is left open to a certain extent. It is often worthwhile to allow two or three groups to improvise on each and to allow time to discuss the varying outcomes of each, before returning to the script itself. The benefit of this approach is that students now approach the script itself with renewed insights from the improvisations.

Another way of using parallel improvisations is to reset the entire action elsewhere, with the possibility of an alternative outcome. This has been done with *Romeo and Juliet* in the form of *West Side Story*. Could it also be set in

Northern Ireland, South Africa or Alice Springs? *Julius Caesar* could be reset in Washington 1963, or Canberra 1975, and *Macbeth* perhaps in the Vatican. Students are asked to improvise using whatever elements of the action they require and to find parallel characters and situations. Discussion would centre around comparison and contrast of all the elements, leading back to close examination of the text.

There are possible follow-up activities, including a drafting of the improvisation into script form, journal writing and newspaper reporting of the incidents as well as writing tasks which focus on the text itself.

Improvisation Based on Characters – The Missing Scene

This use of improvisation calls on students' knowledge and perception of characters in the play and seeks to strengthen their individual interpretations. Basically it asks students to improvise as a particular character in a scene which has happened off stage. The students are stimulated to ask how would this character behave in such a situation. For example in *A Midsummer Night's Dream* students could be asked to improvise the scene between Egeus and Hermia which led to Egeus dragging Hermia before Theseus. They might improvise the scene in *The Taming of the Shrew* where the servant is sent to summon the three wives for their husbands. Students might again experiment with several improvisations, discussing the features of each in terms of the play's presentation of the characters, as well as the ways in which some information about these offstage scenes are incorporated within the text. They might test out the missing scene by inserting their most satisfactory improvisation into a reading of that portion of the play. Discussion could centre on the effects of the omission or inclusion of such a scene. (See also 'Missing Scene'.)

Improvisation Based on Lines – Quotable Quotes

These activities are designed to assist students to formulate a critical stance in relation to the ideas or themes of the play, while at the same time extending their experience of the drama.

Basically key lines, such as "To be or not to be", "Nothing will come of nothing", or "The quality of mercy is not strained", are extracted from the text, and used as the basis of a number of improvisation situations. Discussion following these activities then focuses on comparison and contrast with the text, and a linking up of the ideas of the play with these key phrases (which make ideal quotes for the later writing of 'lit crit' essays).

Solo Improvisations

Quotable quotes can be effectively used as a Just a Minute game. This is based on the BBC word game. A student is given a quote and required to speak for one minute, without hesitation, deviation or repetition on the idea suggested by the quote. This is followed by discussion of the issues, and perhaps a noting of the position of the quote within the context of the play.

Quotable quotes can also be used to improvise in the manner of a homily. Here, a student is given a quote and required to speak as if from the pulpit, a homily based around the given text.

Quotable quotes can also be used as headlines. A student in role as newsreader is given a quote as a headline and required to improvise the accompanying story as if for a television news bulletin.

Other similar situations could be devised based on the use of the quote in solo improvised situations. Follow-up written activities could be devised along the same lines. The quote, for instance, could be subtitle for an editorial encouraging the student to write a piece of discursive prose.

Group Improvisations

First line improvisations: two or three students could be given the quote as the first line of an improvisation. No discussion should precede the improvisation, but discussion of the issues, as well as characters and action and issues should follow.

Last line improvisations: again, two or three students are given the quote, but this time it is to be the last line of the improvisation - ie: the line which ends the scene. It may be advisable to allot the line to a particular student, although after students are familiar with this sort of activity this may not be necessary. Again, no preceding discussion allowed, but reflection upon the action afterwards.

Improvisation based on line: here each group is given a line and asked to develop a short scene based on the line, but not speaking the line. Discussion time is allowed beforehand, although students are encouraged to develop a short scenario rather than to work out detailed speeches. Each group then presents their scene to the rest of the class, whose task it is to work out what the line might have been. The value of this particular exercise is that the students learn to translate verbal imagery into dramatic action, and to explore the subtext of lines, while at the same time exploring the significant ideas and themes of the play.

Improvisation Set Within the Text (see also 'Alter Ego')

In this activity there are a number of possible approaches. One way might be for the teacher to outline the action of a particular scene under investigation. Students then improvise the speeches keeping as close to the outline as possible. This is then followed by a moved reading of the text itself. Having experienced the flow of the action the students are more easily able to deal with the language and to transpose it into the action sequence which they have already experienced.

Another way of using improvisation based within the text is to allot groups of students segments of scenes. Each group is asked to read the segment carefully and then to develop a dramatised version of the scene using their own words. This is presented to the class followed by a dramatised reading of the original text. What very quickly tends to become obvious to the students here is that the language, as Shakespeare has written it, plays a large part in establishing the rhythm of the scene.

A further adaptation of improvisation from the text also involves doubling of roles. Two students elect to play each character. One set stays off stage. These are the voices. They read aloud the lines from the text. The other set are the character's actions. They remain onstage. They must listen carefully to the read lines and perform appropriate actions, gestures and interactions. Again this works best with short units, and is particularly useful to explore the inter-relationships between two characters.

Improvisation can be simply applied within a dramatised reading where a student or students may be struggling with the reading aloud of a complex or long passage. Here the student is asked to read the passage silently and improvise on the passage. The reading or dramatisation is then resumed. This enables students to move more quickly through some of the more convoluted passages, particularly those which have a plethora of metaphor catalogues. It can be explained that such catalogues were appropriate and worked well on the large stage, but can be bypassed on a smaller space without too great a loss of rhythm or meaning.

In several of the Shakespeare Workshop series, improvisation and role play are used as a means of highlighting the issues (and perhaps demonstrating their relevance to young people today) before the study of the play is commenced. See **HV** (Activity 1), **JC** (Activities 1, 7), **KL** (Activity 20), **MAA** (Activity 3), **MND** (Activities 7, 8), **MV** (Activity 2), **OTH** (Activity 1), **RJ** (Activity 1), **TN** (Activity 1), **TS** (Activity 2), **HIV** (Activity 6), **MSS** (Activity 1), **RWT** (Activity 1).

Intercutting

To highlight aspects of character, it is occasionally useful to have students, in groups, try intercutting two sets of lines, eg: in *King Lear*, intercutting Edmund's professions of regard for his father with lines from the soliloquies (I ii) where he reveals his true feelings. See **KL** (Activity 2). See also **Subtext** (Glossary), **RIII** (Activity 13).

Interior Duologue (see Alter Ego)

Interviews (see Also Hot Seat)

In **MAC** (Activity 2) there are suggestions for casting interviews. One member of the group is the actor wanting to secure a particular role, and the others are the interviewing panel. The unit contains a useful casting report form. See also **KL** (Activity 15), **RIII** (Activity 20).

Jigsaw Cloze (see also Sequencing)

A jigsaw cloze works in much the same way as a jigsaw puzzle, except that the pieces consist of the lines of a particular speech. Ideally this will be a monologue or soliloquy, although it may also work with a duologue. Students in groups are given the cut-up lines of the speech and work to construct the speech as they think the character would have spoken it. In doing so they need to consider the character's viewpoint, as well as the poetic or prose form.

Journal

Students can be invited to keep a response journal in which they record their thoughts, feelings, predictions as their study of the play progresses. Not only can this be very informative for the teacher, it also allows students to trace the ways in which their feelings about characters change as their reading of the play progresses.

Another kind of journal, frequently used by actors when preparing to play a part, is the **role journal**. In such a journal, an actor might reflect on his/her feelings as the role is developed over time, or the journal might be used to create a 'biography' when the actor starts answering questions-in-role, such as *What is the best/worst thing that has ever happened in your life?*. (See also **Hot Seat**.) Another dimension can be added by having actors in their role preparation write imaginary letters/memos/notes to other characters in the play. (Reference: Roslyn Arnold, "Managing Unconscious and Affective Responses in English Classes and in Role Plays", *English in Education*, Vol 27 No 1, Spring 1993.)

Journal activities are to be found in **HV** (Activity 2), **KL** (Activity 19), **MAA** (Activity 1), **MV** (Activity 1), **RJ** (Activity 19), **TN** (Activity 5), **RIII** (Activity 3), **MWW** (Activity 1).

Kaleidoscope

This is an activity developed by Brenda Pinder (see **HAM** Activity 3) to help students become accustomed to the language of Shakespeare. The teacher prepares a number of cards (for a class of twenty-four there might be three sets of eight) on each of which is written a line from the play that is about to be studied. The lines chosen should not make specific references to characters or places. The cards are given out to the students who spend a little time exploring in their minds ways in which their line could be said. Then they walk around the room, and every time they pass someone they say their line to that person in a different way.

The next stage is to divide the class into groups matching the sets of cards and ask each group to develop a short scene using those eight lines and no others (except, possibly, a linking word or two). They may set it in a school, or a cafe, or a courtroom; there may only be two or three characters, or everyone may have speaking parts. A fifteen minute preparation time is generally all that is needed. The results are sometimes amazing. See also **TN** (Activity 1).

Mantle of the Expert

Mantle of the Expert, or Enactment of the Expert, involves endowing students with a role that is essentially an "expert" role, and posing a problem in relation to the text or the situation within the play. Students then engage in an activity that involves researching, discussing, enacting from within the expert role. The expert role may be one outside the text, such as an anthropologist exploring the mores of ancient Rome and Egypt, as revealed through the play *Antony and Cleopatra*. It may also be a role within the play's world such as a Friar or Doctor exploring the inner feelings of Hamlet or Romeo etc.

Mime (see Dumbshow)

Missing Scenes (see also Bystanders; Imaginative Recreation)

a.   Directors and actors often seek to influence the audience by adding on scenes or parts of scenes that do not involve dialogue; for example: Sir Henry Irving inserted an extra, wordless scene into *The Merchant of Venice* with the aim of creating sympathy for Shylock (see **MV** Activity 17). Since many scenes in Shakespeare begin "midstream" (eg: the opening of *Antony and Cleopatra*) there is ample scope for students to devise action, noise etc, which will indicate what has gone on before. In the case of *Antony and Cleopatra*, the **tone** of Philo's opening words will be determined very much by what the class imagines must have gone on beforehand.

b.   All the plays offer opportunities for imaginative reconstruction of gaps in the text. See **MAA** (Activity 15); **MAC** (Activity 8), **MV** (Activity 17), **RJ** (Activities 6, 8), **TEM** (Activity 6), **TS** (Activity 7), **RIII** (Activity 14), **AYL** (Activity 10).

Mock Trial

After students have read a play, a mock trial is often an effective way of getting them to marshal evidence for and against a particular character. **KL** (Activity 8) recommends a mock trial of Goneril and Regan. See also **HAM** (Activity 16), **TEM** (Activity 7), **RIII** (Activity 17). In **MSS** (Activity 20), the activity takes the form of an inquest; in **MM** (Activity 22), it is in the form of a Royal Commission.

Model Making

Students can be encouraged to make a model of the stage and using chess pieces or stick figures to represent differing characters can experiment with various blocking plans for particular scenes. Some students could then read key lines and others move the pieces over the stage area. This is the way some directors actually begin to make their own blocking plans prior to rehearsals. (See p105 for details of a Globe Theatre model kit.)

Newspaper/Radio Reports

Useful improvisation and writing activities can be based on the idea of reporters as eye witnesses writing accounts for their journals, or attending press conferences at which the leading characters give their views, eg: **AC** (Activity 17), **HV** (Activity 13).

Music

Not only are there constant references to music in Shakespeare's play (eg: *Twelfth Night*), there are many scenes in which music, singing and dancing play a significant role. Among the classroom activities that suggest themselves would be the choosing of appropriate background music for key scenes, or even the composing of new settings for some of the songs. Follow-up activities after a play has been completed could include listening to excerpts from operas based on Shakespeare's plays (eg: Verdi's *Otello* and *Macbeth*, Gounod's *Romeo and Juliet*, Britten's *A Midsummer Night's Dream*) and to Cole Porter's *Kiss Me Kate* (based on *The Taming of the Shrew*). Mendelssohn's incidental music for *A Midsummer Night's Dream* and the ballets of *Romeo and Juliet* composed by

Tchaikovsky and Prokofieff are all readily obtainable. Berlioz's 'dramatic symphony', *Romeo et Juliette*, is one of his most popular works.

See **MA** (Activity 6), **MND** (Activity 14), **MV** (Activity 16), **OTH** (Activity 18), **RJ** (Activity 3), **TEM** (Activity 10), **RWT** (Activity 14 – *Winter's Tale*), **AYL** (Activity 13).

Obituary

The writing of an obituary for a major character is a good follow-up activity. See **MSS** (Activity 11).

Pastiche Poem

The idea here is to take a key theme from the play (love, say, if the play were *A Midsummer Night's Dream*) and then for the group to find a number of single lines about that theme and then arrange them into a poem. See **MND** (Activity 4), **RIII** (Activity 9).

Program Notes

Theatre programs often contain notes written by the director about his/her conception of the play. A good revision activity is for students, in groups, to prepare a director's program notes, highlighting the thematic and other elements that the group's ideal production would stress. See **HIV** (Activity 21), **MWW** (Activity 22).

Posters

The activity of designing posters for a play, or for the film based on the play, can encourage students to think of those elements of the play that deserve emphasis or that would attract an audience. See **HV** (Activity 18, sheet 2), **RIII** (Activity 21).

Productions and Performances

Extensive records exist of great productions and great performances of the past, and some of these accounts have been woven into the activities in some of the volumes of the Shakespeare Workshop Series. See, for example, **HAM** (Activity 23), **JC** (Activity 19), **OTH** (Activities 6, 19, 20), **HV** (Activity 9), **RJ** (Activity 14), **MV** (Activity 24), **TN** (Activity 24), **TS** (Activity 17), **AYL** (Activity 16), **RWT** (Activity 5 – *Richard II*).

Prompt Copy

This valuable activity requires a group to focus on a key scene and produce a prompt copy, giving instructions to the actors regarding tone, gesture, movement, and instructions to the stage manager about lighting effects, music etc. It could well follow a blocking (qv) exercise. See **HAM** (Activity 23), **JC** (Activity 10), **TEM** (Activity 27), **TS** (Activity 6).

Radio Script

In **RWT** (Activity 7 – *The Winter's Tale*), David Nicholson harks back to the radio serials of bygone years, and suggests that groups write short radio scripts for a series called *Shakespeare's Half Hour*.

Reconstruction

This activity involves taking a key scene in a play and transferring it to a modern setting (eg: Parliament House). Speeches from the play are then translated into the new setting, with whatever adjustments are necessary. See **HIV** (Activity 7), **RIII** (Activity 19).

Role Play (see Improvisation)

Sculpting

This is a technique that uses students as models for characters in the play. The 'model' student is sculpted by the sculptor to represent the character at a particular point in the play, and the position is frozen for a few minutes.

There are a number of ways of using the sculpting technique. It can, for instance, be used to recount the sequence of events in the play from the differing perspectives of key characters. A number of students - say six or seven - may elect to be the models for the character and others become their sculptors. The teacher may recount the key moments where this character is featured, highlighting the character's feelings, mood, and actions. Each sculptor arranges the model to interpret this moment. For Lear, these moments may be Lear dividing his kingdom, rejecting Cordelia, angry at Goneril, out in the storm, reunited with Cordelia and discovering her death. Each model position is held so that there is a visual picture of the sequence. This can then be repeated for other characters, say Goneril, Cordelia or Kent. There may need to be some modification of the instances. Basically what the students are establishing is a picture of the journey that each character makes in the play.

Rather than the teacher recounting these moments the students in pairs can be given the relevant textual references to read prior to sculpting. Thus they are required to make their own decisions about what is happening to the character at this point in time.

If you are fortunate enough to have a drama department with a costume box, you may take in some additional visual props - for example, a crown, a cloak, a dagger and so on, as appropriate. You may also be fortunate enough to have ready access to a Polaroid or other camera. Photographs of each sculpture could become the basis of a storyboarding exercise, or could be mounted on the wall, or in an album with matching textual captions.

The sculpting exercise can be repeated for a number of characters so that differences in perspectives are highlighted. It can also be used so that not only one character is sculpted, but two interacting characters could be traced throughout the play. Characters such as Macbeth and Lady Macbeth, or Romeo and Juliet could be appropriately handled in this way.

Sequencing (see also Jigsaw Cloze)

An activity designed to get students used to the language before commencing the play. Students, in groups, are given a speech in which the lines have been printed out of order. They are then asked to rearrange the lines in the correct order. See **KL** (Activity 13), **MND** (Activity 18), **MV** (Activity 8), **RJ** (Activity 2), **TN** (Activity 6), **TS** (Activity 3). A novel variation of sequencing is to be found in **HAM** (Activity 2).

Set Designer

Placing students in the role of stage designer is a very valuable activity. Stress that before set designs are undertaken decisions have to be made about the type of stage to be used (thrust stage, proscenium arch) and the period in which the play is to be set. (A very successful production of *As You Like It* was set in outback Australia in the 1920s.) **HAM** (Activity 11), **HIV** (Activity 22), **KL** (Activity 16), **MAC** (Activity 7), **MV** (Activity 19), **OTH** (Activity 13), **MM** (Activity 19).

Shakespearian Insults

Like Kaleidoscope (p50), this is an activity to help students become familiar with the language of Shakespeare. A number of insults can be drawn, either from the play to be studied (eg, **MWW**, Activity 2), or from a range of plays. A useful source is *Shakespeare's Insults* by Wayne Hill and Cynthia Ottchen (London: Vermilion Books, 1991), though oddly enough it omits the best insult of all:

> *The devil damn thee black, thou cream-fac'd loon!* (**Macbeth**, V iii)

Each student is given a card on which an insult is printed. After memorising the insults, the students move around the room. And every time they pass someone they say the line in a different way (eg, humorously, viciously, etc).

Spider Charts (see Character Profiles and Spider Charts)

Storyboarding

This is a useful device, particularly where a class is reticent to perform, or where space is restricted. It still emphasises the visual elements of the play and enables students to experience the cinematic nature of Shakespeare's plays.

The links between the shape of each storyboard picture and the shape of the stage become obvious to the students and they are able to explore not only what the stage can do, but also come to understand the characteristics of camera shots in determining meaning. The closeup camera shot, for instance, with the audience looking in on an intimate moment is the equivalent of a scene played in either down stage corner, and long shots with their greater degree of personal distance are the equivalent of scenes played well up stage.

In storyboarding, students often work well in pairs, or groups of three. Groups larger than this tend to be less successful as the focus tends to be lost.

Storyboarding consists of the creation of a picture frame account of the action. Unlike a simple cartoon it indicates by the size and shape of the picture within the frame how the action could be shot with a camera. It is a pictorial representation of the three dimensional frames already described. Each frame is captioned with the words spoken by the character or characters within the frame.

Ideally the entire play could be divided into units, a common style of graphics adopted and distributed to all members of a class. The result would be a complete 'instant play' in picture book form. In practice this takes considerable organisation. However, it is not to be discarded as a device. It can be employed for smaller segments of the play, and is useful for those scenes where there are a number of entrances or exits or some complex action. Again, the value of this activity is that individual students are only asked to confront a small segment of the text for close reading. They are using the text for a pleasurable (and ostensibly simple!) activity. They have the benefit of the close reading done by the rest of the class, and thereby gain an overall picture of the play's action. In practice, they are also encouraged, and do in fact, read more of the text for themselves, spurred on perhaps by the success with which they have managed the reading of their own segment, and the recognition of lines from the segments presented by other members of the class.

See **HV** (Activity 17), **MAA** (Activity 19), **OTH** (Activity 21), **TN** (Activity 16), **TS** (Activity 14).

Tableau (see also Freeze Frames)

Tableau is a means of freezing moments in a script in order to examine what is happening at that moment. It allows a close examination of relationships between characters as evidenced by the proxemic relationships. Tableaux can be set up in groups in the classroom. Time should be set aside for the reading of each tableau.

Captions

This can be enhanced by asking the "audience" to caption the tableau. Several possible captions should be discussed.

Thought Balloons

The teacher or conductor of the tableau can move into the tableau and ask the audience to read the thought balloons for particular characters. The teacher indicates this by drawing an imaginary thought balloon above the head of the indicated character. These thought balloons should be discussed by the audience.

Speech Balloons

The teacher or conductor can move into the tableau and ask the audience to provide the speech balloons for particular characters. The teacher indicates this by drawing imaginary speech balloons in front of the mouth of the indicated character.

Speaking Diary

From the tableau one character may remain while others move away. This character may then speak aloud to the audience his or her feelings about this moment or other events that have preceded the moment. The convention is that the character begins by indicating with the hand that he or she is writing in a diary. This movement then fades away as the character continues to reveal his or her feelings, hopes, wishes etc.

See **TN** (Activity 21). A variation is to create a tableau capturing the most significant issue in a scene, as in **MND** (Activity 16), **RIII** (Activities 4, 10).

A variant on this idea is a tableau representing a wedding photograph (**TS** Activity 18), or tableaux designed as family photographs (eg: of the Montagues and the Capulets).

Two-Handed Soliloquy

Some soliloquies can be turned into a dialogue between the two halves of a character's mind and hence are ideal for pair work. See **MSS** (Activity 6).

Video (see Film Script.)

Writing (see also Film Script; Imaginative Recreation; Journal; Missing Scenes; Obituary)

The Shakespeare Workshop Series contains many suggestions for writing. See **MAC** (Activity 10), **MND** (Activity 5), **TEM** (Activity 2).

In **RWT** (Activity 2), Catherine Radcliffe suggests that a useful activity for a history play like *Richard II* is for the students to construct, using the opening chorus in *Henry V* as a model, a speech such as Shakespeare might have used to explain to his audience the necessary background to the play.

The Globe Theatre

PART B

A

Shakespeare

Festival

Jesse Hise

Stratford on Avon

Introduction

This section of *Shakespeare: A Teacher's Handbook* draws on the expertise of an American teacher, Jesse Hise, who for a number of years ran an ever- expanding Shakespeare Festival at his school. He writes:

> *We started a festival at my school because we hoped the students would see Shakespeare as more than another boring, hard-to-understand writer. We felt we could make Shakespeare **live** for today's students if we could get them involved in activities other than classroom reading.*

Classroom Festival

Hise suggests that you may have to make a small beginning with a festival based on your own classroom, but that once it is seen to be successful, the idea can be sold to other English teachers and eventually become an all-school event. Certainly other classes from the same year level can be invited as audience, and their enthusiasm will help spread the idea. Hise argues that ...

> ***What really counts is visibility.*** [If it is to be held in an ordinary classroom] *the festival must make a difference in the way your classroom looks. It must make a difference in the way the students speak as they practise Shakespeare's words. And it must make a difference in how the students dress - Elizabethan-style costumes will be one of your most successful devices.*

He recommends arranging seating to allow performance on a thrust stage [see Figure 2], decorating the outside of the classroom door as entrance to the theatre [see Figure 1], selling food (in Shakespeare's time the usual foods sold would have been fruit and nuts) and perhaps including an Elizabethan-style puppet show. He writes:

> *The puppet shows could be folk stories ... or you could use puppets to present [shortened versions of] Shakespeare's plays. Puppet shows are especially good for those students who need to hide behind a curtain, where they project their feelings and words onto the puppet.*

Figure 3 shows how to make the stick puppets used in Elizabethan times. Obviously, prime place in the festival must be given to Shakespeare's words: condensed scenes, soliloquies, sonnets, even an entire play. Many of

FIGURE 1.

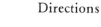

Directions

1. Cover both sides of the classroom door with butcher's paper with some kind of wood grain design. Do somthing similar with the door frames.

2. Make shield type signs for each side of the door along with other

FIGURE 2

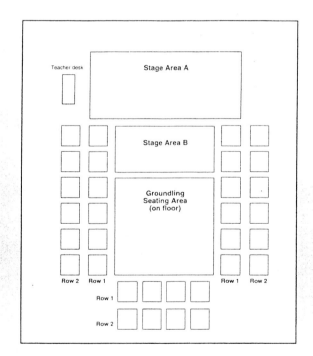

Stage Area A: Here can be found the props and scenery and the main dramatic action.

Stage Area B: Here the actors speak their lengthy speeches or soliloquies. Actors may also move from Stage Area A into this area while the dramatic action is taking place.

Groundling Seating Area: Row 1 Members of the audience sitting here pay two extra pennies.

Row 2 Members of the audience sitting here pay one extra penny.

Shakespeare's plays contain scenes that can stand on their own. Hise suggests the funeral scene from *Julius Caesar* (III ii), the Cinna scene that follows it, or the scene where Macbeth and Banquo encounter the witches (*Macbeth* I ii).

Figure 3: Clown Doll

Directions:

1. Make a clown doll such as is detailed below.

2. By moving and twisting the control stick up and down, you can make the clown bow, hide, jump up, and so on.

3. **Note well:** The entire clown should be able to "hide" in the cone.

1/4 inch dowel rod

old doll's head stuffed ...
... or stuffed fabric

fabric attached here all the way around

arms stuffed with cotton

loose fabric

decorative trim

felt covered corrugated cardboard

2 feet

open end

To these may be added:

- The 'rude mechanicals' scenes from *A Midsummer Night's Dream*
- The 'tricking of Malvolio' scenes from *Twelfth Night* (see **TN**, Activity 11).
- The 'Gadshill' scenes from *Henry IV, Part 1*.
- The Trial Scene from *The Merchant of Venice*.

(See "Cut Versions" in Chapter 4.)

Many of the ideas listed below for larger festivals can be incorporated in a festival confined to a single class.   *KW*

Larger Festivals

Midfest
In a 'midfest', during each hour or so of the day, students from other classes come to your festival area. Set up four or five activities of from six to ten minutes each, and at the trumpet fanfare, students move to a different activity. For example, they could see [a scene] of a condensed play, watch a juggling show and perhaps practise juggling themselves ... watch puppet shows or go to food booths or Elizabethan flower band booths. This approach allows great flexibility in casting of performances and duties, giving more students the opportunity to participate.

All School Festival
What makes the all-school festival different from the classroom festival and the mid-sized festival is that one of the major goals is your attempt to entice **every** student in the school into participating in some aspect of the festival.

The various activities for an all-school festival are simply too much for one person to plan and carry out. You must have a number of teachers who are interested in the project and willing to work; otherwise, you will go stark, raving bonkers in short order.

You also need student help. A special Shakespeare Festival club will be useful. You can call it Jesters and Jugglers, the Shakespeare Festival Club, The Renaissance Club, or any name you and students prefer. The club will be your training ground for the various festival activities. This is also a place to get more than one teacher involved as sponsor.

The beauty of an all-school festival is the developing co-operation you will get from among the various departments in the school. High schools are sometimes a loose confederation of departments eagerly rushing toward their own goals, but not too willing to show concern for goals from elsewhere on the campus. Something like a Shakespeare festival will get teachers working together and integrating the various aspects of knowledge that we feel are important to students.

How do you select what to do for an all-school festival? Start with something very showy – a Costume Day, for example, or running various contests through the English classes and giving the winners school-wide recognition.

Above all, **get Shakespeare performed** – in the classroom, on the auditorium stage, during special assemblies, etc.

Suggestions

In an all-school festival, the participation of teachers from every department is essential. You, as the organiser, should be prepared to show other teachers how to participate and to give suggestions.

First, offer costume ideas well in advance of the festival. Give those who sew an opportunity to prepare their own costumes. Have a list ready of rental places for those who are simply going to go out and rent a costume. Showing drawings of specialised areas of dress – the average person, specific occupations, and so on, might get a wider participation by non-English teachers.

Use the Timeline (pp.69-72) to get ideas to offer other departments regarding Renaissance people who influenced history. I have tried to create a varied list for that section that might open possibilities to other departments. You may wish to duplicate these Timeline pages for interested faculty members.

Here are other suggestions that might help.

1. Invite **any department that wishes to participate** in a Shakespeare exhibit. If enough participate, you might even change the name to the Renaissance Exhibit or something like that. Ask the science department to prepare a display of, say, typical medical treatment during Shakespeare's lifetime, or an exhibit on the plague, or an exhibit on Elizabethan medical beliefs that we would call superstition or ignorance today.

2. The **art department** could prepare the graphics for the entire exhibit, giving the exhibit a professional look. If photography is taught (and most schools at least have a yearbook), the yearbook or photo club could prepare the instant picture taking during the exhibit. And, of course, the art department could prepare an exhibit on the state of art in Shakespeare's time:
    - ❀ Who purchased art?
    - ❀ What was it like?
    - ❀ Who were the great artists?
    - ❀ Did the common person have much exposure to art?

3. The **industrial arts department** could manufacture your exhibit stands and dividers. They might wish to prepare an exhibit on some of the very skilled artisans that existed in Shakespeare's time – some of the crafts we have since lost.

4. The **home economics department** could get involved with costume making. At our school, if the festival can furnish the money, the clothing teacher frequently purchases the material and costumes are sewn by students who cannot otherwise afford to purchase materials for their own projects. Thus, they learn how to sew and we benefit by having more costumes.

5. If there is a **cadet corps** in the school, get them involved with Elizabethan soldier costumes.

6. The **physical education department** could get involved, particularly if you have a tumbling team. Again, in appropriate costume, they could be part of the entertainment on Costume Day. They could research the type of event that might take place at an Elizabethan street fair and present those. Well, maybe not bear baiting!

7. The **social studies department** could prepare exhibits on Elizabethan history, including the explorations to America. They could also focus on social customs in the wide sense:
    - • Who was in prison?
    - • How did they get there?
    - • What crimes were punishable by death?
    - • What laws were enforced that must have influenced Shakespeare?

8. The **music and drama department** of course, can really be helpful. Elizabethan music (wooden recorders are readily available, if you can find the funds) adds to Costume Day and to the banquet. The music teacher can prepare Elizabethan music, both folk and formal. Fanfares could announce events, both on Costume Day and at the banquet. The drama teacher could become heavily involved, but get on his/her schedule well in advance! If the students are advanced enough, they might be willing to tackle a Shakespeare play. If not, perhaps scenes. If not that, specially written light presentations, perhaps satirising some of Shakespeare's famous scenes.

9. The **maths department** members are usually hopelessly addicted to their lesson plans, but perhaps you could at least get them into scholars' outfits. (See costume suggestions.) And check the Timeline entries for mathematical advances during Shakespeare's time.

10. If you have a **special education department** that works with learning disabled students, emotionally handicapped, and so on, do include them. Many teachers may want to use class time to help students enter the T-shirt contest or one of the other contests. Or help students with a costume. You might also want to include these teachers in your video schedule.

11. **Foreign language department** members may be willing to translate Shakespeare into other languages and perform short scenes.

If you can find appropriate suggestions to offer other teachers and other departments, you will find that many are quite willing to join in. **And don't forget your various school secretaries, clerks, and aides**. Many of them will be delighted to join in on Costume Day by dressing appropriately if you get the information to them in time for them to plan.

A Shakespeare Exhibit

A Shakespeare exhibit to coincide with the festival is a useful and educational part of the festivities. This exhibit will aid your festival in at least three ways:

- It will give students practice in planning a display that presents information pertinent to Shakespeare.

- It will give students an opportunity to display the results of their projects and contests.

- It gives teachers a chance to take their classes to an on-campus "museum" tour.

Timeline:
Shakespeare's Life and Times – Selected Events

This brief timeline has been compiled mostly to give you ideas for involving non-English teachers in your festival. It suggests to them important people in their area who were alive during Shakespeare's time.

The items from Shakespeare's life are some of the documentary evidence, court records, house purchases, business dealings, and so on, that are on record. Because it is difficult to know exactly when each of the plays was first produced, I did not include that information.

Shakespeare's birthday is unknown. He was baptised on April 26, 1564. April 23 is traditionally celebrated as his birthday. He died on April 23, 1616.

1564   William Shakespeare is born. Michelangelo dies.

1565   St Augustine, Florida, is established by the Spanish as the first European settlement in North America. Peter Bruegel the Elder paints "Hunters in the Snow".

1566   One of the world's first newspapers is published in Venice.

1567   The Solomon Islands are discovered by Spanish explorer, Alvaro Mendana de Neyra.

1568   Jesuit missionaries visit Japan.

1569   Shakespeare is five years old. The first part of a Spanish epic on the conquest of Chile, *La Araucana*, is published.

1570   The Japanese open the port of Nagasaki to overseas trade.

1571   Jesus College, Oxford, is founded.

1572   Massacre of St Bartholomew kills an estimated 50,000 French Huguenots.

1573   The first German cane sugar refinery is established in Augsburg.

1574   Shakespeare is 10 years old. The University of Berlin is founded.

1575   Plague sweeps through Sicily and Italy.

1576   Francois Viete, French mathematician, introduces the use of letters for quantities in algebra. First theatre is built in England.

1577   Francis Drake sets out to circumnavigate the world.

1578   The catacombs of Rome are discovered.

1579   Shakespeare is 15 years old. Sir Francis Drake sails into San Francisco Bay and proclaims English sovereignty over New Albion (California).

1580   Montaigne, great French essayist, publishes his *Essays*.

1581   Galileo discovers the isochronous swing of the pendulum.

1582   Shakespeare marries at age 18 to Anne Hathaway, age 26. University of Edinburgh is founded.

1583   Shakespeare's daughter Susanna is born. English explorer Humphrey Gilbert annexes Newfoundland and founds the first English settlement in the New World.

1584   Walter Raleigh establishes colony on Roanoke Island. Shakespeare is 20 years old.

1585   Shakespeare's twins, Hamnet and Judith, are born. The first time bombs are used by the Dutch.

1586   Sir Francis Drake attacks and burns St Augustine.

1587   Virginia Dare, of Roanoke settlement, is first English child to be born in North America.

1588   Thomas Harriot's description of Virginia urges further settlement. Shakespeare joins his parents in a lawsuit to recover some property.

1589   Shakespeare is 25 years old. First knitting machine is invented.

1590   Shakespeare begins to produce plays.

1591   Sir James Lancaster becomes first English person to reach East Indies via the Cape of Good Hope.

1592   Shakespeare is 27 years old. First records of Shakespeare receiving income as a playwright. First critical reference to Shakespeare as playwright. The ruins of Pompei are discovered.

1593 London theatres are closed down a year because of plague. Christopher Marlowe, dramatist, dies in a tavern brawl. Shakespeare publishes *Venus and Adonis*, establishing his reputation as a poet.

1594 Shakespeare is 30 years old, publishes *The Rape of Lucrece.* Thomas Nash publishes one of the first English novels, *The Unfortunate Traveller.*

1595 Walter Raleigh explores 300 miles of River Orinoco in South America with four ships and 100 men.

1596 Galileo invents the thermometer. Sureties of peace (peace bonds) filed against Shakespeare and others. (No one has discovered how or why Shakespeare was involved with these people who seemed to be having a sort of feud.) Shakespeare on list of those who were behind in their London taxes. He eventually paid up - in 1600.

1597 First opera, *Dafne*, is performed in Italy. Shakespeare purchases the largest house in Stratford. (We must assume that Shakespeare is doing quite well financially from his work as playwright and other business ventures.)

1598 Lope de Vega, Spanish novelist, writes *La Dragontea*, an epic poem about Sir Francis Drake. Survey shows Shakespeare owns corn and malt in Stratford, indicating he was engaged in either business or speculation or both.

1599 Shakespeare is 35 years old. The Globe Theatre opens. References of the time show that by now Shakespeare has written at least twelve plays: *Two Gentlemen of Verona, Comedy of Errors, Love's Labour Lost, Love's Labour Won* (since lost), *Midsummer Night's Dream, Merchant of Venice, Richard II, Richard III, Henry IV, Titus Adronicus,* and *Romeo and Juliet.* The New World has an estimated 900,000 black slaves.

1600 Smoking and chewing tobacco becomes popular in London.

1601 Shakespeare purchases 107 acres of farmland near Stratford. Also purchases a cottage there.

1602 First successful abdominal surgery is performed in Prague.

1603 Queen Elizabeth dies.

1604 Shakespeare is 40 years old. Johann Kepler publishes *Atronomieae Pars Optica*, in which he explains the workings of the human eye. Shakespeare makes more investments in Stratford.

1605 *Don Quixote*, by Cervantes, is published in Spain.

1606 *Macbeth* is performed for the first time.
Dutch under Willem Jansz sail into Gulf of Carpentaria.

1607 Jamestown, Virginia, becomes first permanent English settlement in New World.

1608 More English settlers arrive at Jamestown, whose original contingent is down to forty people.

1609 Shakespeare is 45 years old. His sonnet sequence, written many years before, is published. Tea reaches Europe from China.

1610 First textbook on chemistry is published by French scientist, Jean Begun.

1611 Danish army adopts rifle for service.

1612 John Rolfe introduces tobacco growing to Virginia.

1613 Globe Theatre burns down.
Dirck Hartog lands on the coast of Western Australia.

1614 Shakespeare is 50 years old.
John Napier, Scottish mathematician, discovers use of logarithms.

1615 Coin-in-slot vending machines for loose tobacco are introduced into British taverns.

1616 Shakespeare dies. Cervantes, author of *Don Quixote*, dies.
Galileo is threatened with torture and death by the Inquisition.

Using Shakespeare's Language

Elizabethan Language

You can add to the spirit of your festival by encouraging students and teachers to use appropriate Elizabethan words and phrases. Here are some with definitions for their use. Some of the words listed have more definitions than the meaning given, but I have selected a common Elizabethan use. Of course, you will notice that many of the words are used differently today and that some are still used, if not commonly, in their Elizabethan meaning.

Where I felt it would help, I have used the words in sentences to help students get started.

Terms of Address

Sir	general male respectful form of address.
Madame or **dame**	general female respectful form of address.
Sirrah	male form of address used for one below your social station or age, such as master to servant, older person to young person, employer to employee, teacher to student.
Lord	respectful male form of address for members of royalty, some governmental officials, and others associated closely with royalty.
Lady	respectful female form of address for members of royalty and others closely associated with royalty.
Your Majesty, Your Highness	respectful form of address used only for the King or Queen.
Thou	*Thou* and *thy* were used as familiar terms of address to family and friends, or older people talking to children. (Similar to the French and Spanish "tu".) If you want to be Elizabethan, teachers may use this form of address with students, but students must be more formal with teachers. That is, they must address them as "sir" or "madame".
Cousin, coz	term for any relative beyond the immediate family such as uncle, brother-in-law, even cousin.
Wench	term of familiar address, applied mostly to serving women. Not really impolite unless applied to royalty or other member of a high social standing or with someone older than oneself. You would not refer to the Queen (or a teacher) as a wench, unless you wanted to lose your head!

Wretch	term of endearment for a child, but when used to an adult, a term of mild contempt, especially for someone who has done something unkind.

General Words

Do not hesitate to combine words and phrases for a better Elizabethan effect, such as "saucy wretch" or "Shog off, post haste, thou proper-false knave. I've had enough of your skimble-skamble."

Amiss	calamity, misbehaviour. Use in place of "What's wrong?" or "What is amiss?"
Ape	to imitate or mock. Use instead of "Are you making fun of me?" (by imitating my talk, my words, my walk and so on.) "Dost thou ape me, knave?"
Attend	listen to, apply oneself. "Students, please attend to my words."
Avaunt	be gone away. Instead of "Please leave this area," say "Avaunt thee, sirs."
Back-wounding	backbiting, gossiping about someone. Instead of "I heard you were talking about me," say "Have you been back-wounding me?"
Baked meats	food in pastry. Instead of "I'll have the chicken pie" say "I'll have the baked meats."
Barber-monger	frequenter of a barber shop, therefore used by the Elizabethans to mean a conceited, vain person. Monger was frequently added to the end of words to mean a person who is excessive. A food-monger eats too much. A fashion-monger is too concerned about clothing, and so on. You can make up your own "monger" words.
Behoove	benefit. Instead of "It would be in your best interest to pass this test," say "It could behoove you to pass this test."
Beslubber	smear. "Do not beslubber you clothes with mud."
Bodykins	A mild exclamation. Use instead of saying something nasty.

Bounteous	liberal, generous. Instead of saying "Thanks, Miss, for passing me," say "O most bounteous madame, thank you for your grace."
Buss	kiss. "Woulds't thou buss me, gentle lady?"
Candle waster	bookworm.
Charge	direct, command, order. "I charge thee, candlewasters, to do thy homework."
Chop	crack in the skin. "In this cold weather, do you have chopped lips?"
Cross	obstruct, challenge. Instead of "Don't try to stop me" or "Don't argue with me" use "Don't cross me on this."
Egg	worthless, inferior.
Enow	enough.
Ergo	therefore.
Et tu, Brute?	You, too Brutus? Not really an Elizabethan expression, but Shakespeare used it in *Julius Caesar* at the moment that Caesar's good friend, Brutus, stabs him. It is now used as an expression indicating a friend's betrayal.
Example	used as a verb. Instead of "Here is an example of a new problem", say "I'll example you with a problem."
Fain	glad, pleased, also willing. "I would fain have some baked meats for dinner."
Fancy free	not in love.
Fecks	a very mild exclamation. Literally means "faith." "Fecks, I dropped my pencil."
Gentle	good mannered, cultivated.
Go to	exclamation meaning incredible. "Go to, you certainly did not buss the Queen in her chambers."
Grammercy	thanks, thank you. (Originated from "God have mercy.")

handsomeness	decency, good conduct.
hie	hurry. "Hie thee to class on time."
Hugger-mugger	secrecy.
Hurly-burly	commotion. "Bodykins, Wilt thou stop this hurly-burly and do thy reading of the lesson?"
Iron-witted	unfeeling, lacking in emotion. "This iron-witted rascal ... ."
Knave	boy servant. Since boys were considered to be full of tricks and jokes, "knavish" means "horsing around". A term used to express mild annoyance. "You knave, didst play a 'Kick Me' sign upon my back?"
Late-walking	keeping late hours. "If thou didst not late-walk so regularly, thou wouldst have thy homework."
Mess	dish or course of food. "What mess didst thou have for lunch?"
Nit	egg of a louse, therefore used as a term of contempt. (Note that today we still use the term "nitwit", which means the person has the brain of a louse.)
Peevish	silly or obstinate. "You peevish knave, stop throwing thy books on the floor."
Perchance	perhaps; can also mean "by chance". "Perchance I will get an A on the test."
Pleaseth	please it or "Does it please (you)?" Pleaseth you for me to close the door?"
Post haste	with great speed, "Sirrah, convey this cheque post haste to the bootmaker."
Proper-false	handsome, but false-hearted.
Quoth	used as "said". "Who is this peevish wretch?" quoth I.
Ready	used as "here" or "present" in answer to your name being called.

Shog	go away. "Shog off, knave, and leave me."
Sick-thoughted	love sick.
Saucy	insolent. "You saucy knave to say that I am cruel and mean when I am really sweet and kind."
Skimble-skamble	nonsense, confusing. "I was trying to understand the balance of power, but it was skimble-skamble to me."
Tarry	stop, stay, wait for. "I will tarry here until the warning bell ringeth for class."
Zounds	a mild exclamation. "Zounds, this test is difficult."

Quotations from the Bard

Shakespeare's phrases can be used in many ways during a festival. How we use a quotation is limited only by our imaginations. Any display and use of Shakespearean phrases makes the language seem more natural, more beautiful, instead of something aged and foreign to the students.

Suggestions

1. Print shorter quotations on posters, banners, buttons, and note pads.

2. Longer quotations can be used, especially in a classroom size festival. Students first memorise and deliver the quotation, then explain its meaning and implications.

3. If you have a midfest or all-school festival, a quotation contest can be held beginning a few days before the festival. The first students to identify the play and/or the character who spoke the lines get free admission to the festival, or another form of recognition.

4. Using phrases on buttons or carefully crafted cardboard pieces around 7 x 12 cms (which can be given as prizes) is a good way to promote the goals of the festival and the goals of teaching Shakespeare. For example, use certain quotes from plays which would arouse curiosity of students who are not familiar with that particular work. "Alas, poor Yorick" ... "Et Tu, Brute?" ... "Where's Polonius?" ... "Wherefore art thou Romeo?" ... "Hail, Thane of Cawdor!"

5. Another way to use buttons of cardboard pieces, particularly, is to use phrases that are "all purpose", those phrases that someone might want to say to another, or about him/herself. Examples are: "Sweets to the sweet!" ... "Give the word" ... "Are we not brothers?" ... "Love is merely a madness" ... "The world's my oyster" ... "I have had a most rare vision."

6. If you schedule festival activities on March 15, you can always advertise "Beware the Ides of March!".

7. When using quotations, it is a good idea to cite the play, act, and scene. On buttons, this may be too difficult because of their small size, but on large items it is useful to cite the source. That not only gives name identification to Shakespeare's plays, but you will be surprised how many times students really want to know where the words came from.

Selected quotations

This list of quotations doesn't even begin to scratch the surface of the possibilities, but it will help you get started.

"There's small choice in rotten apples." *Taming of the Shrew*, I i.

"Why, this is very midsummer madness." *Twelfth Night*, III iv.

"Lord, what fools these mortals be!" *Midsummer Night's Dream*, III ii.

"I dote on his very absence." *Merchant of Venice*, I ii.

"My library was dukedom enough." *Tempest*, I i.

"Every man can master a grief but he that has it."
Much Ado About Nothing, III i.

"There was a star danced, and under that I was born."
Much Ado About Nothing, II i.

"A goodly apple rotten at the heart." *Merchant of Venice*, I iii.

"I have had a most rare vision." *Midsummer Night's Dream*, IV i.

"All the world's a stage ..." *As You Like It*, II vii.

"Fie, what a spendthrift he is with his tongue!" *Tempest*, II i.

"... for tis the mind that makes the body rich." *Taming of the Shrew*, IV iii.

"Misery acquaints a man with strange bedfellows." *Tempest*, II ii.

"Why then, the world's my oyster, Which I with sword will open."
Merry Wives of Windsor, II ii.

"O brave new world that has such people in 't." *Tempest*, V i.

"The quality of mercy is not strained ..." *Merchant of Venice*, IV i.

"Boys, apes, braggarts, Jacks, milksops!" *Much Ado About Nothing*, V i.

"Love is merely a madness." *As You Like It*, III ii.

"It is a wise man that knows his own child." *Merchant of Venice*, II ii.

"What's in a name? that which we call a rose
By any other name would smell as sweet."   *Romeo and Juliet*, II ii.
"Men's eyes were made to look ..."   *Romeo and Juliet*, III i.
"Beware the Ides of March!"   *Julius Caesar*, I i.
"I love the name of honour more than I fear death."   *Julius Caesar*, I ii.
"He doth bestride the narrow world like a Colossus."   *Julius Caesar*, I ii.
"It was Greek to me."   *Julius Caesar*, I ii.
"A dish fit for the gods."   *Julius Caesar*, II i.
"Cowards die many times before their deaths,
The valiant never taste of death but once."   *Julius Caesar*, II ii.
"Let slip the dogs of war"   *Julius Caesar*, III i.
"Mischief thou art afoot!"   *Julius Caesar*, III ii.
"The seeds of time."   *Macbeth*, I iii.
"This is a sorry sight."   *Macbeth*, II ii.
"Something wicked this way comes."   *Macbeth*, IV i.
"Take thy face hence."   *Macbeth*, V iii.
"To thine own self be true."   *Hamlet*, I iii.
"Something is rotten in the state of Denmark."   *Hamlet*, I iv.
"This is the very ecstasy of love."   *Hamlet*, II i.
"What a piece of work is man! How noble in reason!"   *Hamlet*, II ii.
"O, what a noble mind is here o'erthrown."   *Hamlet*, III i.
"The lady doth protest too much, methinks."   *Hamlet*, III ii.
"Alas, poor Yorick!"   *Hamlet*, V i.
"Sweets to the sweet."   *Hamlet*, V i.
"The rest is silence."   *Hamlet*, V ii.
"Beware, my lord, of jealousy ... It is the green-ey'd monster .."   *Othello*, III iii.
"My salad days when I was green in judgement."   *Antony and Cleopatra*, I iv.

Costume Day

Every festival needs at least one chance for all students to dress up and play a part, even if it just means walking around all day to class as an Elizabethan.

For a classroom festival, not only the actors need the opportunity to dress – the audience should be Elizabethans also. For the all-school festival, Costume Day will be the only event some students will participate in. It is the lure which makes the festival visible; it is the opportunity to show the sceptics that Shakespeare can be fun.

Costume day can be enlivened with a grand parade of all the participants in the day's festivities: jesters, musicians, actors, puppeteers, fortune tellers and so on. The school choir can perform songs from Shakespeare's time, and the teacher or dance teacher (if you are lucky enough to have one, or can persuade a dance teacher from outside the school to help) can stage Elizabethan folk dances.

The festive atmosphere can be added to if the decorative half-masks used in Renaissance times (see Zeffirelli's film of *Romeo and Juliet*) are made (and perhaps sold as a way of building up funds for future festivals), if pies and tarts are sold, and if quotation buttons are sold.

Costume day is your opportunity to make sure that every student in the school, whether or not he/she chooses to participate, knows that there is definitely something special going on, and that William Shakespeare (dead or alive!) is somehow connected to it.

Costumes: Plain and Fancy

How deeply you go into costuming and how ornate the costumes will be depends partially upon the economic circumstances of your students. Your costume activities should avoid becoming a type of competition in which students feel they must spend tons of money.

Costumes **do**, however, help a festival, large or small. Having at least one day in which as many students as possible wear a costume brings a type of involvement that builds from year to year.

Making costumes

For your students to make costumes, they will need time, patterns, and at least a little money. Time won't be much of a problem, for if your students are interested, they'll find the time to work on their costumes. Finding costume patterns, however, can be a problem. Direct them to the illustrations in this book and to the many they should find in your school library's books on historical costume. Also, if possible, order several copies of Winter and Savoy's *Elizabethan Costuming For the Years 1550-1580*, (Other Times Publications, Oakland, California). We have found it immensely helpful for designing costumes for our festivals. Many of the various types of costumes discussed in this section are clearly illustrated in Winter and Savoy's book. Finally, most costumes or costume materials cost some money, although the expense can be quite small. As mentioned above, remember to be sensitive to your students' economic situation.

Interestingly enough, money for clothes was important to the Elizabethans, too. The dress of Elizabethan society heavily depended upon one's social-economic class. Some types of clothing were reserved for the court, and the newly rich of the middle class had to pay a fee for permission to dress in certain types of clothing resembling royalty.

Key terms

One way to handle the situation at school without using terms such as lower class, middle class, and so on, is to use the following terms:

Military	Since armour was still in some use (and armour is difficult to simulate) military dress can be simulated by using a tunic type outfit with some sort of symbol of the King (lion, crest, cross, and so on) in the middle of the front. Tunics are also a good all purpose costume, even though they are more appropriate, perhaps, to an earlier century. But they are easy to make, compared to other types of costumes, and can often be made from clothing purchased at opportunity shops.
Village and farm	These would be the everyday outfits of those who work the fields or with their hands. The work clothing would reflect their trade.
Merchant and town people	This clothing would be of greater quality and in more abundance than those of the village and farm people, and the styles imitate but not rival the royal trends.
Royalty	This collection of clothing is the most colourful and most ornate, including fancy accessories.

Also remember that you are striving not necessarily to achieve authenticity (unless you have a large budget) but to give an Elizabethan effect, a feeling among your participants that they are in another era. It's easier than you might think.

Tunics

If you have home economics or sewing classes (and some money), you could have someone make tunics. Tunics were still in use but did come from a previous century. They, however, are fairly easy to make and, when worn with tights or tied-down jeans, look great. Tunics can be made large enough to simply slip over the student's regular clothing, so if you have students who come by public transport and want a costume to put on easily at school, tunics fill the requirement.

Tunics have puffed sleeves, made with drawstrings at the wrists. The neck portion of the tunic is also made with drawstrings to simulate the frilled collar effect that was so popular with the Elizabethans.

Military tunics

Military tunics are quite similar to a regular tunic. Most noticeably missing, however, is the neck portion which is ordinarily used to form the frilled neck. Such a neck portion is definitely out of place on the battlefield! Sleeves are still full, though the sleeves not necessarily go to wrist length. Sometimes under the tunic men wore leather or metal for protection. The king's emblem often appeared in the middle of the chest area.

The royal or court dress – male

Imitating royal dress does have its problems, but outfits for males can be easily obtained if the youth uses imagination.

First, tights. When first starting a festival, all boys, without exception, swear by the grave of Henry VI that they couldn't wear tights. Don't fight it. What will probably happen, even the first time you do a festival, is that a couple of boys will show up in tights, loudly proclaiming that they look like fools and worse, but their teacher is giving them extra credit. The next year, more boys will show up dressed in tights. I can't explain it – it just happens.

However, tights are really necessary only if the student chooses to wear the short, puffed breeches, sometimes called "slops". (Admittedly, tights would be more stylish and therefore virtually required form of dress for a male at court.) These are puffed, not because of some early form of starch, but because they stuffed them to make them puff out. These can be made fairly cheaply by purchasing drawstring trousers at an opportunity shop, cutting them off around the knee, and sewing elastic at the bottom.

Most males will wear the longer, below the knee length breeches, resembling the old knickerbockers. Knee length stockings would then be quite adequate.

If possible, there should be ribbons above and below the knee. These not only helped keep the tights from sagging; they were also considered quite fashionable for their own sake.

Any puffed sleeve shirt would work, particularly if it had some ornate pattern that gave an Elizabethan effect. A plain waistcoat could help complete the outfit.

The fancy neck collars can also be made cheaply from ruffled material. Simply take the material, circle it around the person's neck, and fasten with a couple of safety pins. It looks amazingly authentic.

Hats can be avoided completely, or send the students to used clothing stores of any kind. Many, many styles of women's hats from the past fit the Elizabethan look, particularly if you go to a craft store and pick up a feather for each hat.

Capes are optional, but they can be designed from an old blanket, edged with fake fur.

Shoes are fairly easy for the royal class. Modern-day loafers or house slippers do just fine. A fancy bow on each would even be better.

Royal or court dress – female

The dress for women isn't all that difficult, either, except in decoration. Ornateness was the rule of the day as you can see from the illustration.

What are the requirements for imitations? First, long sleeves are a must. No decent Elizabethan woman would show her elbows. A puffed sleeve would help. The skirts must be long, the bodice usually tight. A considerable amount of trim was used.

Hats were not as ornate as the men's hats. You could use any fairly small, plain hat decorated and trimmed.

The general rule for dressing like one of the royal group is "the most decorative, the better." Of course, no one was permitted to dress in a manner that would appear to outdo the Queen!

Merchant and city – male and female

Middle class people simply imitated the styles of royalty. Naturally, their clothing was plainer and, as today, would sometimes combine a fairly simple pair of tights with a more ornate waistcoat. The collar would not be worn as frequently, except by those closely associated with royalty or other wealthy people.

Middle class women still wore the long skirts and long sleeves – those items cut across class lines, but their clothing was simpler and less ornate.

So, in producing a festival, whether in the classroom or for the entire school, students can wear the same basic outfit. Only the degree of ornamentation need change.

Village and farm – male and female

In many cases, this group would contain the poorest people, but obviously we want to avoid making Costume Day a contest of higher, middle and lower economic classes.

However, modifying modern clothing to fit the village and farm classification is the easiest outfit to make to produce an Elizabethan effect. To imitate tights (and possibly for convenience of hard labour) loose fitting trousers of the time were tied, at least from knee to ankle. Jeans adapt well to this treatment. Heavy twine works well to tie them. Tied jeans and a loose fitting shirt would be all a male needs for a costume. Many of today's collarless shirts give an Elizabethan look.

For the females, long, full skirts and long sleeves are again appropriate. Use nothing ornate. These people worked hard around the farm. Aprons were commonly worn many hours of the day and tight fitting bodices were frequently worn over the loose fitting blouses.

Contests

In addition to Costume Day, contests form the basis of the goal of involving as many students as possible in the festival. The contests are the lure to get students to learn and use Shakespearian language.

Festival poster design contest

To build a festival from year to year, one activity that will generate competition and interest is the festival poster design contest.

It has certainly helped us to have the co-operation of one of the art teachers. With her assistance, we developed a list of guidelines for the students entering the contest. We decided on the wording we wanted on the posters. The art teacher decided, knowing the materials and her students, what the rules would be that affected the process of reproducing the poster.

We sometimes give cash prizes, sometimes gift certificates at a local art store, and of course, the winning poster is reproduced to be distributed in every classroom of the school three weeks before the festival.

T-shirt design contest

In this particular event, the student must select a phrase from Shakespeare, draw it onto a t-shirt, and then appropriately illustrate it. The illustration may be satiric, serious, ironic, humorous, or simply decorative.

The student must furnish a t-shirt. Many times students bring in outgrown shirts. Perhaps you could find a source to purchase either factory rejects or heavily discounted t-shirts to enable the students to wear their design on Costume Day. You will probably want to display your top prize winning designs, however, in the Shakespeare exhibit for the week of the festival.

Liquid embroidery and cloth paints work fine. Try to get donations to fund a supply of these for teachers who are interested in making this a class project. Some students will pool money and buy four or so basic colours and share them.

We also furnish a list of some Shakespeare quotations, especially if a teacher is having an entire class enter the contest. (See Quotations from the Bard.)

Greeting card contest

This contest is similar to the t-shirt contest. Students select a Shakespeare quotation that would be appropriate for specific occasions when they would probably send a special card: *Thank You, Birthday, Mother's Day* and so on.

These cards could also be simply to advertise the festival itself or note cards with a Shakespeare quotation on the outside and blank space for writing on the inside.

The contest could be designed to give prizes in the various greeting card categories, or simply for the most creative cards. At the end of the judging when cards are returned, students would be encouraged to actually send their card to someone.

Perhaps a design would arise which would be appropriate and of high enough quality that you might want to consider having the card printed and used as a fundraiser for the festival.

Here are some possible quotations for cards. Your students can find many more, I'm sure.

Thank you

"I can no other answer make, but thanks, and thanks, and ever thanks
..."   *Twelfth Night*, III iii.

Congratulations

"Is it not well done? Excellently done ..."   *Twelfth Night*, I v.

"O wonderful, wonderful and most wonderful, wonderful! And yet
again wonderful, and after that, out of all whooping!"
                                                       As You Like It, III ii.

Wedding congratulations

"A contract of eternal bond of love,
Confirm's by mutual joinder of your hands,
Attested by the holy close of lips ..."   *Twelfth Night*, V i.

"God, the best maker of marriages,
Combine your hearts in one ..."   *Henry V*, V ii.

Love and friendship

"I know no ways to mince it in love,
but directly to say "I love you ..." *Henry V*, I ii.

"Love alters not with his brief hours and weeks." *Sonnet* 116

"Did my heart love till now? Forswear it, sight!
For I ne'er saw true beauty till this night."
                                                       Romeo and Juliet, I v.

"We two alone will sing like birds i' the cage."   *King Lear*, V iii.

"How like a winter hath my absence been from thee ..."
                                                       Sonnet 97

Birthday

"Tell him he wears the rose of youth upon him."
                                                Antony and Cleopatra, III iii.

"His years but young, but his experience old;
His head unmellow'd but his judgment ripe."
                                               Two Gentlemen of Verona, II iv.

"O call back yesterday, bid time return ..."   *Richard II*, III, ii.

"And send him many years of sunshine days ..." *Richard II*, III ii.

Bon voyage

"Let him spend his time no more at home,
Which would be a great impeachment to his age,
In having known no travel in his youth ..."

Two Gentlemen of Verona, I iii.

Sympathy

"His life was gentle, and the elements
So mix'd in him that Nature might stand up
And say to all the world, 'This was a man!' " *Julius Caesar*, V v.

"... tears shall drown the wind ..." *Macbeth*, I vii.

These quotations are simply intended as samples. You and your students can find dozens of such phrases from Shakespeare to use in this manner.

Recitation contest

Getting students to recite Shakespeare is one of the exciting events of the festival. For a few weeks, it becomes respectable to memorise Shakespeare!

We usually run two contests, a solo and a group contest. In the solo contest, the student memorises a set number of lines and recites them. We have used a fifty-line maximum in the past. The goal is that the student would give a recitation that clarifies the meaning of the lines.

Writing contest

One goal of the festival is to arouse more interest in Shakespeare and his time that might result in students actually visiting the school library to find out a little more about Elizabethan times.

To accomplish this, you could sponsor a special edition of the school newspaper. If your school has no newspaper, publish one of your own.

The writing in the newspaper would focus on the festival, on Shakespeare, on Elizabethan times, and on a fictional use of Shakespeare and his characters. You could have a Dear Willy column, in which the advice that Shakespeare gives on human relationships would have to include at least one appropriate quotation from one of his plays. There could be fictional, but historically based, descriptions of the London plague, a visit to an Elizabethan theatre performance, a story of an apprentice who sneaks away from an afternoon of theatre at the Globe, a discussion among the City of London (council) about the evil influence of plays and what actions they take, a picture of going to grammar school in a small town such as Stratford-upon-Avon. You could have poetry about Shakespeare and his plays, both serious and humorous.

Use humorous classified ads such as, "For Sale: Like new dagger, 6-inch blade, silver with black handle, 60 shillings. Contact Macbeth, North Dunsinane 2014."

Create serious news articles also, with headlines such as "Plague threatens London", "Fire destroys Globe Theatre", "Shakespeare reported dying; revises his will".

How many categories of writing you would want to judge would depend on how many teachers you have to help. Perhaps the prize winning writings would simply be those that are selected and published in the newspaper and/or magazine.

If Shakespeare performances are available, live or on video, your newspaper could include reviews of them.

Costume Contest

As a featured part of Costume Day, you will want to recognise various categories of costumes, especially if you are trying to build your festival from year to year. Here are some suggested categories:

1. Best royal costume, male.

2. Best royal costume, female.

3. Best costume using contemporary clothing modified to give an Elizabethan effect.

4. Best common person costume.

5. Best specialised costume (jester, military, occupational).

Any contest will do!

These ideas are suggestions to get you thinking about what might be appropriate for your school. We are always thinking of new contests to try.

Our goal is always the same: **Get as many students as possible involved in some aspect of the festival** – reading, speaking, and hearing Shakespeare's language.

Elizabethan Banquet

From the first year of our Shakespeare Festival, the Elizabethan banquet clearly was on its way to becoming the hit of our annual festival.

The banquet is one of the best opportunities to get parent and community involvement in your festival. If you are starting out without much experience, I recommend that your first banquet be for students only. You need to have a "trial run" to see how all the activities are going to work.

One can call the banquet anything. It should be a combination of food and entertainment. We refer to ours as the Elizabethan Frolic. Other schools call theirs the Elizabethan Feaste. But what's in a name, as someone once said.

What to Serve

From my reading about Elizabethan cooking, serving a truly authentic Elizabethan meal would probably cause everyone to become ill. Only the upper classes had much meat, and with the conditions of storage, much of the spoilage of the food was disguised with heavy spices. On the royal level of earls, dukes and kings, the banquets could become ridiculously ornate. Some were fond of taking a large animal, such as a cow, stuffing it with a smaller animal, and on and on until perhaps a pigeon was the smallest animal inside, so that when the monstrosity was served, animal would be produced from animal to the apparent delight of the crowd.

I don't think you want to do that at **your** Elizabethan banquet.

Fresh game, of course, was served to the upper classes. That, too, is a problem. So I recommend going fairly plain. Serve beef, pork, or lamb - roasted. Baked fish was also served. They did use rice and vegetables. Fruit was frequently a dessert (still a European custom today). Cheese was used, especially baked in crusts or bread.

In preparation, if you want to be reasonably authentic, simply ask yourself, "Could the Elizabethans have done this?" Kiwi fruit, for example, was probably among the missing items in an Elizabethan diet.

The more simple the meal is, the less in cost and preparation time. Unless you are able to charge a ticket amount that will actually cover expenses (and so far we haven't been able to do this at my school), you need meals that don't require a chef.

For one of our banquets, we served the following: roast pork (whole pigs turned on a skewer outside the banquet area), roast chickens, lettuce and tomato salad, shepherd's bread with cheese baked in the centre, selection of fruit, apple juice, and cherry tarts.

The roast pig and chicken, along with the salad, was catered. Admittedly, the modern roasting cart looked a bit out of place, but the pigs turning on the spit were quite impressive. Our shepherd's bread was obtained by the parents of a couple of our students who run a sandwich shop. They obtained the bread from one of their suppliers, who cut the price drastically when told it was for an Elizabethan banquet. They also obtained the fruit at very low cost. Our own district vocational school supplied the cherry tarts at a reasonable price.

The apple juice was used for the constant toasting to the King and others that went on during the meal.

You can, of course, recruit teachers to buy and prepare the food, and with the co-operation of suppliers discounting for you, this is probably the most inexpensive way.

How far you go into preparing Elizabethan fancy food would depend upon your own research and how complicated you wanted to get and how much money you had available. *Fabulous Feasts* and *The Magpie History of Food* (see "Useful Books") suggest such items as beef pie, lentils and lamb, beef and chicken pie, and girdle cake. Or how about chicken stuffed with lentils, cherries, and cheese? Artichokes with blueberry rice? Vegetable gruel? With today's teenagers, gourmet tastes fluctuating between one fast food establishment and another, you probably understand when I suggest you keep it plain and simple.

We served buffet style, but hope to work up to having the food served by students in costume, with fanfares of trumpets. No utensils are used. All persons have to eat with their fingers. Of course the Elizabethans had knives and spoons (and even used them sometimes), but we like to insist on using fingers, for it rapidly immerses the audience into the spirit of the evening.

We use paper plates, definitely not authentic, to save on cleanup, but if the banquet keeps developing the way it has, we will someday have our own metal dishes to serve with. Having metal containers to drink from would add to the atmosphere, but then you have problems with storage from year to year, to say nothing of the initial cost.

Decorations

The first rule is to have a large cleanup crew that will work after the banquet is over. That is also the second and third rule.

Then work on the table decorations. Use leaves, flowers, branches, anything natural that could be something possible in Elizabethan times.

Try to get the walls hung with banners and coats of arms. (See the section on Banners for ideas.) But remember that even what we perceive as the ornateness of an Elizabethan royal banquet really depended heavily upon the ornateness of royal clothing, the colourful and dramatic serving of each course, and fanfares rather than quality china and crystal. So work on the audience to come in costume, decorate the walls as best you can, and keep the table settings simple.

Entertainment

The banquet moves along with food being served as various entertainment happenings occur.

Royalty should be present at the banquet. You can have the students elect a King and Queen sometime during the festival before the banquet, or you can select many kings and queens, either at the banquet or before.

Kings and queens are given crowns, of course. You can find reasonably sturdy paper crowns at novelty stores and use them year after year.

If you prefer to have one couple "rule" the banquet, other students could be given titles such as duke, duchess, earl and so on. The King and Queen control the banquet. No one eats till they eat. No one drinks till they drink. Toasts are offered to their health. All entertainers bow to the King and Queen before they perform.

The King and Queen should enter to the fanfare of trumpets. Everyone stands, of course, and bows as the royal couple pass by and approach the head table. Leading them in is a royal escort who carries their coat of arms.

Once at the table, the King (or Queen) states a few words of welcome and bids the guests to be seated. The royal master of ceremonies does the actual running of the entertainment, but always with deference and constant acknowledgments to the King and Queen.

Dukes and earls may approach the king, usually to present a gift or a lavish litany of praise. Dukes and earls could have their favourite entertainer whom they present to the King before the entertainer performs.

Another way of doing this is to have several kings and queens, each with a small kingdom of a couple of tables. They assign various serving tasks, if necessary, and keep the kingdom in order. If you choose to have these various small kingdoms, one of the rules will need to be something like this: No wars or arguments between kingdoms. (Need I say more?)

The meal can be served by having each King/Queen select serving people from among their kingdom to perform the various tasks. Those selected would serve **one** dish or item, then be replaced by someone else. You wouldn't want guests at the banquet feeling they can't enjoy the evening because of being pressured into service!

Another way to do it, however, is simply to get your Shakespeare Club, or other volunteers (such as the English teachers with student help) to plan on "working" the banquet from beginning to end. That way, the servers could truly get into the role of being server, which could be part of the evening's entertainment.

Here are some **specific entertainment ideas**, both light and serious:

1.   Speech contest winners present their monologues.

2.   Persons sing modern songs that relate to Shakespeare, his characters, his plays. ("What a Piece of Work is Man" from *Hair*; "Brush Up Your Shakespeare" from *Kiss Me, Kate*, "Apology" from *Kean*.)

3.   Teachers perform duos or short scenes. These scenes introduce more Shakespeare plus give students a chance to see their teachers in a different role.

4.   Students perform excerpts.

5.   A scene from Shakespeare is put to dance and performed by members of the dance class.

6. Elizabethan folk dances are performed.

7. Jesters perform a monologue comic routine with references to Shakespeare's plays and/or his times.

8. Jugglers demonstrate their skills.

9. Renaissance music is played live or as background music. Particularly appropriate is a classical recorder quartet.

10. Madrigal singers perform.

11. Performers lip-synch and dance to modern pop songs that use Shakespeare's plays or his characters.

12. The famous Wayne and Shuster parody of *Julius Caesar*, "Rinse the Blood off My Toga", can be mimed.

Other program ideas

Since the idea of the evening is to move things along in a rapid, lively way, presenting awards for various Shakespeare festival activities is something you may not want to consider doing.

However, if interspersed with livelier events, it **will** work. Get the costume winners up in front all at one time. That shows students how to get a bit more creative for the following year. (**Make a video recording to show next year's students and to promote next year's fundraising.**)

Closing

The evening should come to some definite conclusion. The King should probably say some final words before he and the Queen are escorted out.

Phrases for Knaves and Wenches

Here are some words and lines from Shakespeare to suggest to your servers for use at appropriate times during your banquet. Most of these phrases are a bit on the saucy side, so remember to tell your servers that when they are serving royalty or other titled persons (duke, duchess, earl, and so on), they should never fail to be polite. Address all such people as lord and lady.

Words
- gramercy – thank you.
- mess – dish of food.
- shog off – go away.
- saucy – insolent.

Phrases
- Be not saucy with me, sirrah.
- Dost thou come here to whine?
- Thou crusty batch of nature.
- What is the cause of your distemper?
- Do not beslubber your clothes.
- I see we have some old crab trees here.
- Men of few words are the best men.
- Let thy betters speak.
- Are his wits safe?
- You tread upon my patience.
- I never did see such pitiful rascals.
- I know his lordship is but merry with me.

Banners and Standards

Banners
Banners can be displayed anywhere around the campus you can find a safe place to hang them where pranksters won't be tempted to remove them.

The purpose of the banners is to give the atmosphere you want – royalty, a different era, whatever.

Standards
Standards were the official emblem of the King or other titled person. Instead of having a square shape, standards were usually tapered, (see illustration) and contained the essential emblem of the titled person, not just colours.

You may want to have students design a standard or standards for your festival or for their own club or organisation to be used during the festival. At your banquet or on costume day activities, groups could participate under their standards.

Standards can be made quite easily and fitted to dowel rods for hanging. Butcher's paper and felt are two materials for the standard's shape. Students can paint the butcher's paper, or they may cut out coloured pieces of felt and then glue them as a design onto the piece of shaped felt.

Ideas for banners and standards

1. Use Shakespeare's coat of arms.

2. Use coats of arms from other Elizabethan royalty or other countries of that era. Check your school library.

3. Use Shakespeare quotations.

4. Students create new coats of arms for their names.

5. Create your own school crest into a standard.

6. Use colourful banners of various sizes in as many places as you can safely hang them during the festival.

BANNERS
Directions

1. Have students make banners for your banquet.

2. The banners should be painted onto butcher's paper.

3. Suggest that your students use strong primary colours.

4. Encourage them to keep their designs simple and bold.

5. Hang the posters around the room to add to the festive air at the banquet.

STANDARDS
Directions

1. Have students make standards for your banquet if you are including a military emphasis.

2. The standard requires a round pole and either butcher's paper or fabric.

3. A coat of arms should be attached to the fabric.

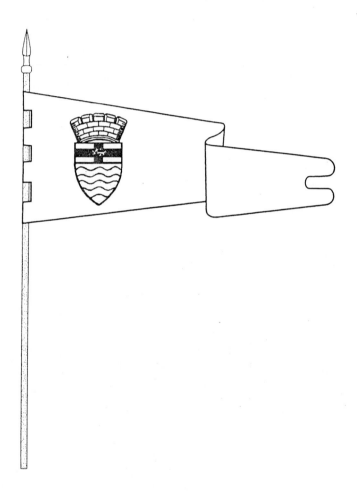

COATS OF ARMS
Directions

1. Students can make coats of arms in two ways:
   a) by painting designs on white butcher's paper;

   b) by cutting up pieces of differently coloured felt and gluing these pieces onto a larger background piece.

2. The coats of arms can then be attached to the butcher's paper or felt standard.

PART C
Resources
and
References

SHAKESPEARE ON
FILM AND VIDEO

"... the ingenious guidance of the camera ..."- Walter Benjamin

There have been many screen versions of Shakespeare's plays. The ones listed here are, in general, the most successful – and the easiest to obtain. In addition to the films listed, there are some interesting Russian versions, notably Kozintsev's *Hamlet* (1964) and his *King Lear* (1971) – difficult to get hold of, but worth the effort. There is also a Japanese version of *Macbeth*, called *Throne of Blood* (1957).

Several of the volumes in the *Shakespeare Workshop Series* have units on particular film and television versions. Such units are clearly indicated under the titles of the films to which they refer. A recent St Clair publication, *Shakespeare on Celluloid*, edited by Neil Béchervaise (Sydney, 1999), provides explorations of the film versions of the following plays: *Hamlet, Macbeth, Julius Caesar, Romeo and Juliet, The Taming of the Shrew, Twelfth Night, Richard III, King Lear* and *Othello*. Films that draw their inspiration from Shakespeare, such as Al Pacino's *Looking for Richard*, are also dealt with in this book, which was short listed for The Australian Awards for Excellence in Educational Publishing.

Studies of Shakespeare on film include:

Neil Béchervaise (ed), *Shakespeare on Celluloid* (see above).

Lynda E Boose and Richard Burt (eds), *Shakespeare, The Movie*, London: Routledge, 1997.

Anthony Davies and Stanley Wells, *Shakespeare and the Moving Image: The Plays on Film and Television*, Cambridge: Cambridge University Press, 1994.

Peter S Donaldson, *Shakespearean Films/Shakespearean Directors*, Boston: Unwin Hyman, 1990.

Charles Eckert (ed) – *Focus on Shakespearian Films* Eaglewood Cliffs: Prentice Hall, 1972.

Russell Jackson (ed), *The Cambridge Companion to Shakespeare in Film*, Cambridge: Cambridge University Press, 2000.

Roger Manvell – *Shakespeare and the Film*, London: Dent, 1971.

Kenneth Rothwell, *A History of Shakespeare on Screen: A Century of Film and Television*, Cambridge: Cambridge University Press, 2001.

Stanley Wells (ed) – *Shakespeare Survey 39*, Cambridge: Cambridge University Press, 1987.

Film Versions

Chimes At Midnight directed by Orson Welles. The story of Falstaff, drawn primarily from *King Henry IV* (Parts I and II) and *Henry V*.

Hamlet (1948) directed by Sir Laurence Olivier. A greatly praised version, but one with some odd features: the voiceover telling us that this is "the tragedy of a man who could not make up his mind" when the film itself does not emphasise such a view of Hamlet's character; the omission of Fortinbras.
Hamlet (1990) directed by Franco Zeffirelli, with Mel Gibson as Hamlet and Glenn Close as Gertrude. Well worth screening.

Hamlet (1998) directed by Kenneth Branagh. This consists of two versions: a four-hour complete version, and a two-hour shortened version. Branagh gives the play a 19th century setting; he himself plays Hamlet, with Derek Jacobi as Claudius, Julie Christie as Queen Gertrude, and Kate Winslett as Ophelia. (See the detailed treatment of the Olivier, Zeffirelli and Branagh versions in *Shakespeare on Celluloid*.)

Henry V. There are two versions readily available: the Laurence Olivier 1944 film and Kenneth Branagh's 1988 version. See **HV** (Activity 20).

Julius Caesar (1953) directed by Joseph Mankiewicz. This film featured James Mason as Brutus, Sir John Gielgud as Cassius, and Marlon Brando as Antony. A highly successful adaptation, particularly interesting for its use of accent to add to the characterisation: Casca speaks in a Bronx accent, while Cassius and Brutus speak with RP English accents.

King Lear (1969) directed by Peter Brook, with Paul Scofield in the title role.

Macbeth (1971) directed by Roman Polanski, with Jon Finch as Macbeth and Francesca Annis as Lady Macbeth **MAC** (Activity 11). A justly popular film with students.

Macbeth (1978) directed by Trevor Nunn, with Ian McKellen as Macbeth and Judi Dench as Lady Macbeth. The acclaimed Royal Shakespeare Company production.

A Midsummer Night's Dream (1999) directed by Michael Hoffman, with Kevin Kline as Bottom and Michelle Feifer as Titania.

Much Ado About Nothing (1993) directed by Kenneth Branagh, with Branagh and Emma Thompson in the main roles. Not to be missed.

Othello (1965) directed by Stuart Burge, with Laurence Olivier as Othello and Maggie Smith as Desdemona. A film of the famed National Theatre production, it illustrates very graphically how different film acting is from stage acting. A great disappointment, but selected scenes can be used. Orson Welles' film of *Othello* has just been re-released (1993) and presumably will soon be available on video.

Othello (1995) directed by Oliver Parker, with Laurence Fishburne as Othello and Kenneth Branagh as Iago. **OTH** (Activity 23). (All three dealt with in *Shakespeare on Celluloid.*)

Richard III (1955) directed by Sir Laurence Olivier. Not as successful as his film of *Henry V*, but certainly worth screening.

Richard III (1996) directed by Richard Loncraine, with Ian McKellen as Richard. A powerful film, set in a 1930s Britain overtaken by civil war and dictatorship. **RIII** (Activity 23). (Both films dealt with in *Shakespeare on Celluloid.*)

Romeo and Juliet (1968) directed by Franco Zeffirelli, **RJ** (Activity 16).

Romeo and Juliet (1996) directed by Baz Luhrmann. A lively version, set in a modern American city, Verona Beach, torn apart by the feuding of rival gangs. **RJ** (Activity 17). (Both versions dealt with in *Shakespeare on Celluloid.*)

The Taming of the Shrew (1966) directed by Franco Zeffirelli **TS** (Activity 15). Elizabeth Taylor and Richard Burton play the main roles.

Twelfth Night directed by Neil Armfield. A witty Australian version. **TN** (Activity 23).

Twelfth Night (1988) directed by Kenneth Branagh and Paul Kafno, with Richard Briers as Malvolio.

Twelfth Night (1996) directed by Trevor Nunn, with Nigel Hawthorne as Malvolio and Ben Kingsley as Feste. This version is set in the late 19th century Austro-Hungarian Empire. **TN** (Activity 25). (All three versions are discussed in *Shakespeare on Celluloid*.)

Television Versions

Note: Unless otherwise stated, the television versions are those produced by BBC/Time-Life TV.

Antony and Cleopatra (1981) directed by Jonathan Miller, **AC** (Activity 25).

Hamlet (1980) directed by Rodney Bennett. Derek Jacobi plays Hamlet; Gertrude is played by Claire Bloom.

Henry IV, Part One (1979) directed by David Giles. Jon Finch is Henry, and David Gwillim the Prince.

Henry V (1979) directed by David Giles, with David Gwillim as the King. While teachers may wish to use some scenes from this version, it is generally considered to be a failure.

Julius Caesar (1979) directed by Herbert Wise, with Keith Michell as Antony, Richard Pasco as Brutus, and Charles Gray as Caesar. Again, some scenes are worth using for purposes of comparison, but the whole is not as compelling as the MGM film (see above).

King Lear (1982) directed by Jonathan Miller. Michael Hordern's performance as Lear provides an interesting contrast with Olivier's Lear (see below); Hordern is always an interesting actor.

King Lear (1983). A Granada Television production, directed by Michael Elliott, with Laurence Olivier as Lear and Leo McKern as Gloucester. Diana Rigg is a "surprisingly reptilian Regan".

Macbeth (1983) directed by Jack Gold, with Nicol Williamson as Macbeth, and Jane Lapotaire as Lady Macbeth. Selected scenes can be used for comparison with the Polanski film.

The Merchant of Venice (1969). Audio-Visual Productions, directed by Jonathan Miller, with Laurence Olivier as Shylock and Joan Plowwright as Portia. Splendid performances and an interesting 19th century setting. Worth seeking out.

The Merchant of Venice (1980) directed by Jonathan Miller. Warren Mitchell is Shylock and Gemma Jones is Portia.

A Midsummer Night's Dream (1981) directed by Jonathan Miller.

Much Ado About Nothing (1984) directed by Stuart Burge. Benedick is played by Robert Lindsay, and Beatrice by Cheri Lunghi. **MAA** (Activity 19, sheet 2).

Othello (1981) directed by Jonathan Miller. **OTH** (Activity 19, sheet 2).

Richard III (1983) directed by Jane Howell, with Ron Cook as Richard.

Richard II ( ) One of the best of the very variable BBC series, with Derek Jacobi giving a fine performance as the King. **RWT** (Activity 3).

Romeo and Juliet (1978) directed by Alvin Rakoff. Nowhere near as good as the Zeffirelli film, but some excellent scenes that are worth screening for discussion and comparison with the film. **RJ** (Activity 16).

The Taming of the Shrew (1980) directed by Jonathan Miller, with John Cleese as Petruchio. Not as lively as the Burton-Taylor film, but well worth screening. **TS** (Activity 15).

The Tempest (1980) directed by John Gorrie, with Michael Hordern as Prospero.

Twelfth Night (1980) directed by John Gorrie, with Felicity Kendal as Viola. Students will almost certainly prefer the Neil Armfield film (see above).

GLOBE THEATRE MODEL

A useful kit for constructing a cardboard model of Shakespeare's Globe Theatre, designed by Heritage Models (UK). In Australia it is available from St Clair Press.

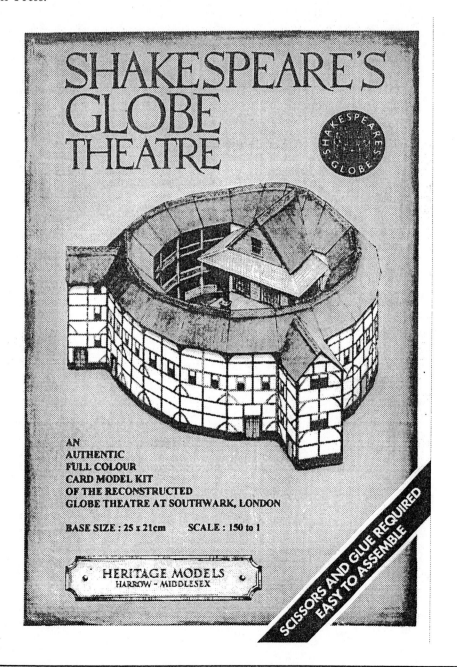

SHAKESPEARE AND THE
NEW TECHNOLOGIES

Anthony Adams

Teachers of Shakespeare have, of course, always embraced the latest technologies in order to enhance their classroom work. First there was Shakespeare on film, already dealt with elsewhere in this volume, which was superseded by videos of Shakespearian films. The great difference between film and video is the greater flexibility and malleability of the latter medium. Videos can be used by a whole class, small groups or individuals; it is possible to freeze frames, to watch in slow or fast motion, to play sections of the tapes over and over again. It is also easy to assemble a library so that the same scene from a play can be viewed in a number of different film productions to enable comparisons to be made between them.

DVD, the latest development in this field which will doubtless soon replace the video in the same way as the CD has replaced the record, while superficially the same in a different and more viewable format, is as different in potential as video was from film. It contains search facilities and is likely to include more than just the 'text' of the film, including out-takes and interviews with the director and cast.

Now, with the increasing use of ICT (Information and Communication Technologies) in schools, the CD-ROM and the Internet have taken over where the video and DVD left off. However there are important differences between the two media. The CD-ROM, though it is even more flexible than a video or DVD and has important characteristics of its own, some of which are listed below, is nonetheless ultimately just another learning resource provided by the school, a modern version of a textbook in fact. It is still limited by the skill of its authors, has a structure of its own which the user can only navigate in certain predetermined ways, and a content that is limited by the ROM's memory. Thus, liberating as it is, students (well familiar with CD-ROMS in their home world) will see it as still rooted in the school curriculum, the learning opportunities afforded by the school.

In respect of the teaching of Shakespeare, a large number of CD-ROMs have been produced (some of the most interesting of which are listed and described below) and they are all likely to possess some of the following characteristics:

1. Text

The ROM will contain a complete copy of the text (often with variants) together with the ability to print the whole of it or extracts. The latter is a particularly powerful application as it enables the easy production of work sheets (eg, cloze exercises), scripts for performance, including individual parts. The fact that the text can be represented in many different ways at the choice of the user (font, size, spacing) is very useful. For example, parts can be produced in a large font enabling easy reading or for use with the partially sighted.

Another text feature of many ROMs is the ability of users to interpolate their own commentary so that the class can build up an electronic dialogue on their appreciation of the text.

Some ROMs will also include a critical apparatus, although the value of this is often somewhat dubious.

2. Characters

There will usually be some thumbnail sketches of the characters but, of much more value, there is also likely to be pictures based upon paintings or productions of how these have been presented on the stage by particular actors or in important productions. Of course this can be done in a conventionally printed book but the advantage of the ROM is the sheer volume of such information that can be incorporated.

3. Plot Outline

There is usually some visual representation of the course of the plot alongside brief plot summaries. This is often helpful to weaker students who have difficulty in remembering what is happening in the play from one study period to the next. A particularly good example of the value of visual representation of plot will be found in the *Romeo and Juliet* ROM listed below.

4. Interviews

A very interesting feature of many ROMs is the inclusion of interviews with well-known actors and directors often as small video clips. There may also be some short extracts from key scenes and productions in the form of video clips.

5. Search facilities

Thus each ROM will contain a vast amount of material, which it would require a whole library to assemble in any other way. The value of this material will of course depend on the quality of the compiler. However the search facility which is built into the ROM's construction should enable this vast mass of information to be accessed easily and quickly. For this to happen the ROM needs to be constructed around some clear principles of 'navigation' and some are much better than others in this respect.

Of particular value is the ability to search the text itself for particular words, word clusters (for example, image exploration), or particular quotations. It is usually also possible to use colour coding for parts of the texts when searched. Thus in *Macbeth* students could mark all the images of blood in red. The ROM can therefore be transformed into a creative medium for students to use in their own learning process.

But, in a sense, the limitation of the CD-ROM is that it is a 'book' (albeit a multi-media book with a very sophisticated index) in a modern form. It is like the jump from illuminated manuscripts to the printed texts of Caxton. In the end it presents a 'text' and that text is fixed.

The internet is quite different in concept and its anarchic nature means that it is infinitely navigable, providing the opportunity for students to have much more control over the pace and content of their own learning. The corollary of this is, of course that the teacher has much less control. It is possible to use the internet with whole class teaching, with projection facilities, but this is by no means the best use of it. It is much better, if more risky, to let students surf the Web for themselves and they will find all manner of unexpected, impossible to predict, outcomes.

The CD-ROM is fixed; the internet changes daily, or even hourly. Thus in the list of resources given later the sites are quoted accurately at the time of writing but may in some cases have changed, or even disappeared, by the time this is being read. However, the bulk of them will remain in use. More importantly, in the process of searching for them, many new sites were discovered, some of which have been included in the list. It can of course only be a brief selection from what is available; where possible, key sites have been listed which will lead the user to other sites which deal more explicitly with what is being searched for.

It is also important to remember that, alongside these latest developments (writing in 2001) there are earlier forms of ICT, which may still have value for the teaching of Shakespeare.

Videodisc

Although these were seen as a very exciting development only a few years ago, they have now been somewhat overtaken by changes in the available technology and few schools will have the necessary videodisc player. This is a pity because a videodisc is like a conventional video but holds a vast amount of material and also incorporates search facilities. It is quite possible to hold on one disc 30 or more complete productions of a play from different countries, cultures and traditions. There are also facilities for viewing the material by zooming in close up together with the usual video fast forward, rewind, and freeze frame facilities. Thus (for example), it would be possible to watch over a dozen representations by different actors of Hamlet's 'To be or not to be.' soliloquy and close in to focus on the actor's face. As a tool it is invaluable, albeit an expensive one.

An important difference between the performances on videodisc and the video clips on CD-ROMs is that, because of the limitations of memory, the clips on ROMs will generally be very short and presented using a technique known as Quick Time which is more like a 'flick book' effect than real video. On the videodisc, by contrast, there are no real memory limitations and the videos themselves will usually be of broadcast quality. They can also be projected for whole class use. Most videodiscs will include the same kind of background material as CD-ROMs but to a much greater extent, given the vastness of memory resources available.

Simulations

The commercial software company, ACTIS, details of which can be found on their Website [http://www.actis.co.uk], has produced a very interesting set of computer-based simulations in their Inquest Series. These give students the opportunity to explore key turning points in some of the most common plays through role play leading to deepening understanding of plot, character, and motivation. Scenarios are presently available for *Julius Caesar, Macbeth, The Merchant of Venice,* and *Romeo and Juliet.* For example, in the *Julius Caesar* inquest, 'the Senate of Rome is to debate the motion: "This House condemns the role played by Marcus Brutus in the assassination of Caesar".' The simulations are exceptionally well designed and the computer (generally two at the most are needed) acts as the game controller. They are all supplied with extensive teachers' notes and work materials for students and have been designed to work with a full age and ability range of students. The software is available for both PC and Apple platforms.

Resources

CD-ROMs

(Nowadays most ROMs will run on both Apple and PC based platforms. It is however always still worth checking whether what you are ordering will also run with the system that you are using. It should also be kept in mind that most are available either as single use or with multiple site licences.)

Shakespeare's Complete Works: This presents a scholarly text of the complete works with ability to print out and with very sophisticated search facilities. As a starting point for developing the use of ICT in the teaching of Shakespeare it is an invaluable starting point for the use of ICT in teaching Shakespeare. Developed by Andromedia Software (USA); distributed in UK and elsewhere by TAG (www.taglearning.com).

Twelfth Night: This was one of the first Shakespeare CD-ROMs to be produced, part of the pioneering Renaissance project based at Ultralab in the Anglia Polytechnic University. It set a standard for what was to follow and is still very useable. Particularly interesting was its navigation device based upon the Globe Theatre, which acted as an index to the ROM's contents, which provide a useful guide to the play and its historical and theatrical background.

Karaoke Macbeth: An interesting though unevenly presented concept in the form of a production of *Macbeth* on ROM where some parts can be cut out of the performance and taken over by members of the class.

BBC/Collins individual plays: These ROMs presenting materials on individual plays produced by the BBC in collaboration with Collins Publishers are brand leaders in this field. They offer a full text in performance with many inter-active opportunities and supporting work sheet materials. At present the following plays are available in the series: *Hamlet, Julius Caesar, Macbeth, Midsummer Night's Dream, Romeo and Juliet,* and *The Tempest.*

Virtual Macbeth (Kar2ouche): This is the first module to be released by Immersive Education working in conjunction with the University of Oxford's Department of Educational Studies. At the time of writing, release copies are not available but the supporting advertising claims that 'audio-visual presentations and printed material can easily be produced by teachers and pupils from libraries of characters, scenes, props, sound effects and audio. In the role of director, users can set and dress scenes, select, create or record dialogue, annotate text, add speech bubbles and special effects'. Available from Immersive Education Ltd (www.immersiveeducation.com).

Internet Sites

Shakespeare: In a way this is the key site that you will need. It is part of a vast collection of Internet Resources under the general title, English Teaching in the United Kingdom. The Shakespeare section is immense with numerous links to all manner of other sites worldwide. If you start here, you can navigate to almost anywhere. The site itself contains resources on many of the plays and much useful background material. http://www.english1.org.uk/shakes.htm

Another such site is www.daphne.palomar.edu/shakespeare/ from North America.

ACTIS: As indicated above, ACTIS pioneered, largely through the work of Chris Warren, the development of computer-based simulations on Shakespeare. It has now moved to important internet developments and, in particular, presents *Shakespeare on Line*, as part of *English on Line*, a subscription service to schools. This is an annual event which enables students taking part to interact with leading performers and each other and to celebrate a week-long engagement with Shakespeare, including video clips of Shakespearean scenes with different interpretation.

http://www.actis.co.uk/shakespeare/

The Globe Theatre: A very large site dealing with both Shakespeare's Globe and the newly reconstructed Globe on the South Bank is maintained by the University of Reading. It is well worth visiting.

http://www.rdg.ac.uk/globe

The New Globe: This is the commercial website of the new Globe on Southbank and has up-to-date details of performances, background material on the plays performed and it is also possible to take a virtual tour of the theatre. Used in conjunction with the previous site it is of considerable interest.

http://www.shakespeares-globe.org/

(With reference to classroom applications.)

Binary Oppositions

Some linguists argue that language – and hence literature – rests on binary oppositions: all concepts are defined by relating them to their opposites, such as life/death, light/dark, hard/soft, male/female. One or two go even further and assert that the first part of a binary opposition is privileged over the other. The idea is sometimes helpful when exploring the patternings and thematic concerns of a play. See **OTH** (Activities 11, 12).

Blank Verse

Shakespeare's plays are written in the standard blank verse line of his day, the unrhymed iambic pentameter (the verse form closest to the rhythms of everyday speech). An iamb is a metrical foot consisting of an unstressed syllable followed by a stressed syllable [∪ /]. The following line is a good example:

∪ / ∪ / ∪ / ∪ / ∪ /
Uneasy lies the head that wears a crown

But Shakespeare constantly breaks up this pattern in various ways:

/ ∪ / / ∪ / ∪ / ∪ /
What a full fortune does the thick-lips owe
∪ / ∪ / / ∪ ∪ / ∪ /
Or hew my way out with a bloody axe

Writing on Shakespeare's poetry in *The Shakespeare Handbook*, Philip Edwards has this to say:

> Strong effects are created by the interchange of verse and prose. Passion or heroism in verse is counterpointed by the realism, commonsense or cynicism of prose, as with Falstaff at the battle of Shrewsbury, or Iago introducing Roderigo to his philosophy of life

... But verse can represent order against disorder, as when at the end of the 'nunnery' scene during which Hamlet has ranted at her in disordered prose, Ophelia (so near distraction herself) laments in measured verse:

> O, what a noble mind is here o'erthrown!

(*The Shakespeare Handbook* ed Levi Fox, Boston: Hall, 1987 p207)

Teachers will find a useful unit on Shakespeare's poetry in **AC** (Activity 24). In **MAA** (Activity 14) there is a discussion of the misleading claim that in Shakespeare the 'high' characters are given poetry to speak while the 'low' characters speak in prose. In **AYL** (Activity 2) there is an activity inviting students to explore the dramatic impact of movements between prose and verse. Other volumes with units on blank verse include **HIV** (Activity 2), **HV** (Activity 3), **JC** (Activity 2).

In **MAA** (Activity 2) there is a unit on Shakespeare's sonnets which can be used in conjunction with any play which has love has a major theme.

See Group Soliloquy (Chapter 4, "A Range of Activities" p.42) for a way of creating awareness of blank verse.

Caesura

A break or pause in a line of poetry, usually signalled by some form of punctuation. See particularly **AC** (Activity 24). See also Chapter 3.

Deconstruction, Shakespeare and . . .

(See also Post-Structuralism)

In her book *Shakespeare in the Classroom* (Open University Press), Susan Leach advocates a deconstructionist approach. She has this to say:

> At its most basic level, one can describe a deconstructionist approach as one which seeks to take the text to pieces to see how it works. This highly simplistic definition is nevertheless useful

works. This highly simplistic definition is nevertheless useful because it enables the teacher to generate a series of questions about the particular text to be worked on, and also allows great freedom to manoeuvre: one can investigate how the text works from any one of a number of perspectives (p89).

Some of the questions she finds useful in generating ideas for deconstructing chosen parts of the text include:

1.   Who holds the power in the play? What is the economic basis of the play?

2.   Is the power upheld/obeyed/challenged/overthrown?

3.   What is the framework within which the play is operating, as indicated by its own internal evidence?

4.   Is it possible to make **easy** judgements about the behaviour of any character?

5.   How does gender work in the play?

6.   How are women presented?

These questions are explored in some detail in the book.

Deixis/Deictic

The deictic features of the language are those words the significance of which is entirely determined by the context, that is, all pronouns and also words like "this" and "that", "here" and "there". Susan Leach, the author of *Shakespeare in the Classroom* (Open University Press) has suggested in her workshops that, as a means of unravelling confusing relationships in a text like *A Midsummer Night's Dream*, a student reading, say, Egeus's speech could point to each of the characters referred to (and to himself when the words "I", "me" and "mine" are used) each time a deictic word is used.

> Full of vexation come **I**, with complaint
> Against **my** child, **my** daughter **Hermia**.
> Stand forth, **Demetrius**. **My** noble **lord**.
> **This** man hath **my** consent to marry **her** ...

Dramaturge

A dramaturge in the theatre usually has a background in both writing and directing. The dramaturge works very closely with the director in the process of production. He or she carries out the research needed for the production, as well as completing aspects such as translation. Translation may involve translation from one language into another, or it may involve translation or transforming of a script for a different historical period, a different stage shape and form, a different theatrical style. Essentially the dramaturge considers how the ideas of the script could be presented in this different context or form.

Enjambment

(Also *enjambement*.) Running on of the sense from one line to the next without any punctuation (in contrast with endstopped lines, where sense and metre coincide in a pause at the end of the line). See **AC** (Activity 24).

Feminist Criticism and Shakespeare

Increasingly, critics of Shakespeare's plays have concerned themselves with the ways in which gender assumptions operate in both the writing and the interpretation of the plays. In her *Reading Hamlet* (Scarborough, WA: Chalkface Press, 1989) Bronwyn Mellor discusses feminist readings of the characters of Ophelia and Gertrude. Catherine Belsey's *The Subject of Tragedy* gives a feminist perspective on a number of Shakespeare's plays. In the **Shakespeare Workshop Series** the volume *Such a Mad Marriage: The Taming of the Shrew* inevitably touches on such issues.

Folio, First and Quarto

In his lifetime, several of Shakespeare's plays were printed in quarto editions. Some of these, known as "Good Quarto" editions, were, it is thought, printed from his own manuscripts. Six were, however, versions probably taken down by dictation from actors, and these are known as "Bad Quartos". Although these 'bad' texts are clearly deficient in many ways, they sometimes have alternative readings that correct errors in better texts. Versions of *Hamlet* and *King Lear* are among the "Bad Quartos". In 1623, seven years after Shakespeare's death, the First Folio edition, comprising all Shakespeare's works except *Pericles*, was published. Later Folios appeared in 1632, 1663 and 1685. *Pericles* first appeared in the Third Folio. Of the four Folios, the First is regarded as the best, as it was put together by James Heminges and Henry Condell, two actors who had known and worked with Shakespeare. Variations between the Quarto and Folio editions of *Othello* are explored in **OTH** (Activity 10). **MM** (Activity 18) explores text changes in *Measure for Measure*.

Fool

The Fool is often a quite important character in Shakespeare's plays, especially *King Lear* and *Twelfth Night*, and his significance is well worth exploring. See **KL** (Activity 9) and **TN** (Activity 15), **TS** (Activity 12).

Imagery

Each play of Shakespeare's has its own patterns of imagery – groups of connected metaphors which work on our imaginations cumulatively. See **KL** (Activity 10), **MAA** (Activity 11 sheet 2), **TEM** (Activity 11), **TN** (Activity 8), **MSS** (Activity 13), **RWT** (Activity 9).

New Historicism

New Historicism describes a range of related assumptions about and approaches to texts. While it is "historicist" in its insistence on the relationships between text and context, it is "new" in its overt political agenda(s) and its cultural relativism. New Historicists subscribe to the following positions:

✿ The production of a "literary" text is enmeshed with material social practices.

- Literary texts are not a special category, but circulate in a network with non-literary texts.

- No discourse – whether literary, historical, anthropological, aesthetic, or whatever – expresses unalterable human nature or universal truths.

- All acts of interpretation are subject to the discursive practices of the society under scrutiny.

A characteristic method is to seize on some surprising anecdote and analyse it in parallel with a focused text in order to disclose the codes of behaviour, structures and ideological assumptions of a whole society. (John Stephens)

The leading "New Historicist" is Stephen Greenblatt, who has written *Shakespearean Negotiations* (Berkeley, LA, University of California Press, 1988).

Post-Structuralism

(See also Deconstruction.) The post-structuralist position, put simply, is that there is no absolute and unchanging standard by which anything (including literature) may be judged; what counts as truth or knowledge is socially constructed – by institutions such as governments, universities, schools. Post-structuralist literary critics seek to investigate the connections between the sources of power and the literature produced. The process of such an investigation is often called deconstruction. Post-structuralist critics of Shakespeare include:

- Malcolm Evans, *Signifying Nothing: Truth's True Contents in Shakespeare's Text*, Brighton: Harvester, 1986.
- Terry Eagleton, *William Shakespeare*, Oxford: Blackwell, 1986.
- Terence Hawkes, *That Shakespeherian Rag* London: Routledge, 1986.
- Terence Hawkes, *Meaning by Shakespeare*, London: Routledge, 1992.

Prose in Shakespeare (see Blank Verse.)

Pun (see Wordplay.)

Quarto (see Folio, First and Quarto.)

Rhyme

When a rhyming couplet is used in Shakespeare's plays, it generally has one of the following functions:

a. To mark the end of a scene or an act.

b. To mark the conclusion of a long speech.

c. To accompany the exit (or occasionally the entrance) of a major character.

Rhyme is sometimes used to mark a change of subject, as when Orsino, in *Twelfth Night*, says:

> *Enough! no more!*
> *'Tis not so sweet now as it was before.* (I i 7-8)

In the early plays there are rhymed prologues and epilogues (eg: the prologue to *Romeo and Juliet*). Where there is a play-within-a-play, as in *Hamlet*, extensive use is made of rhyme. There is somewhat less use of rhyme in the later plays than in the earlier.

A major use of rhyme is the "love sonnet" sequence in *Romeo and Juliet*, see **RJ** (Activity 4).

Soliloquy

Robert Speaight, in *Shakespeare on the Stage* (London: Collins, 1973), writes:

> *The absence of dramatic criticism at the time (of Shakespeare) ... leaves us in the dark about much that we would like to know. What, for example, were the uses of soliloquy? Did the actor begin by talking to the audience, and then, as Shakespeare's art matured, did he increasingly talk to himself? May we not detect a difference of perspective between Richard III telling us frankly that he is going to "play the villain", Viola wondering why Olivia has sent Malvolio after her with the ring, Edmund arguing the natural rights of bastardry, or Iago trying to justify his machinations - and Hamlet in the contemplation of suicide, or*

*Macbeth in the meditation of murder? The perspective would shift easily for the same character in the same play. Hamlet, in his first soliloquy, could inform the audience ... that he is burnt up inside because of his mother's marriage; and, in his last, ask no one but himself "what is a man, if the chief good and market of his time be but to sleep and feed?" ... It was easy to share one's most secret thoughts with the audience under that open sky and in that octagonal arena ... Whether they were spoken **to** the audience or **with** them was a matter of theatrical discretion* (p22).

Wendy Michaels (see Chapter 1) is strongly of the view that the soliloquy should be seen as a dialogue with the audience.

See particularly **HIV** (Activity 9), **JC** (Activity 14), **MAA** (Activity 5), **OTH** (Activity 7), **HAM** (Activity 22), **MSS** (Activity 6).

Sources of Shakespeare's Plays

Shakespeare drew his plots from a wide variety of sources, including Plutarch's *Lives Of The Noble Greeks And Romans* and Holinshed's *Chronicles*. Once students have read a play, it can be informative for them to look at the source material to see how Shakespeare has adapted it to suit his dramatic purposes. See **MAC** (Activity 6), **KL** (Activity 5), **MSS** (Activity 5), **AYL** (Activity 1), **RWT** (Activity 10).

Subtext

A term used for the unspoken or underlying intention of the words, which the actor must imply by tone, pause, emphasis, gesture, facial expression. David Mallick's *How Tall Is This Ghost, John?* (AATE) is full of examples of how the subtext can be explored in the classroom. See **OTH** (Activity 2), **RJ** (Activity 2, sheet 2). See also Alter Ego ("A Range of Activities").

Verse Lining

Shakespeare was adept at using the verse lining to indicate the relationship between actors on the stage. Verse lining has to do with the sharing of lines of the verse between two characters. Sometimes two characters share a single line of verse, as for instance:

Macbeth: *Hath he asked for me?*
Lady M: *Know you not he hath?*

Here the two characters share a single line of verse. The question mark after Macbeth's line acts as a caesura for the line – the cut or break in the middle of the line. The players know that they have a single line and that the caesura should not be a pause.

This type of verse lining is very significant in assisting the players in speaking their lines, and therefore in establishing the relationship between them. In the above example Lady Macbeth is cutting off Macbeth's question very quickly with her answer. There is no moment of pause or contemplation, but simply her very quick curt reply. This establishes the relationship between the two at this stage of the play.

Wordplay

The Elizabethans delighted in wordplay, though a later age all but rejected it. Dr Johnson complained that a pun or quibble was to Shakespeare "the fatal Cleopatra for which he lost the world and was content to lose it". Today Shakespeare's wordplay has been reinstated as a major poetic device. M M Mahood (*Shakespeare's Wordplay* London: Methuen, 1957) argues that "Shakespeare's puns have an active dramatic function ... They may be 'in character' or they may be a vital part of the play's thought." As an example of the former, he instances Mercutio's punning in *Romeo and Juliet*; as for the latter, the word sparring of Katherine and Petruchio, and of Beatrice and Benedick, is an integral part of the plays of which they are the central characters. See **MAA** (Activity 17).

Wordplay is also used to give relief after great emotional tension, as in *Much Ado about Nothing* after Hero has been rejected by Claudio at the altar.

It should be noted that playing on words like *sun/son* and *hart/heart* was part of the stock in trade of most Elizabethan poets.

USEFUL BOOKS

Background Reading

Jonathan Bate, *The Genius of Shakespeare*, London: Macmillan, 1997.

Margreta de Grazia and Stanley Wells, *The Cambridge Companion to Shakespeare*, Cambridge University Press, 2001.

Brenton Doecke (ed), 'Shakespeare in Australia', *English in Australia* No. 125, August 1999.

Norrie Epstein, *The Friendly Shakespeare*, London: Penguin, 1993.

Gareth and Barbara Lloyd-Evans *Companion to Shakespeare*, London: Dent, 1978.

Levi Fox *The Shakespeare Handbook*, Boston: G K Hall, 1987.

John Golder and Richard Madelaine (eds), *O Brave New World: Two Centuries of Shakespeare on the Australian Stage*, Sydney: Currency Press, 2001.

Ivo Kamps (ed) *Shakespeare Left and Right*, London: Routledge, 1991.

Gary Taylor, *Reinventing Shakespeare: A Cultural History from the Restoration to the Present*, London: Hogarth Press, 1989.

Peter Thomson *Shakespeare's Theatre*, London, Routledge, 2nd edition, 1992.

Performing Shakespeare

Philip Brockbank (ed) *Players of Shakespeare I*, Cambridge: Cambridge University Press, 1988.

Russell Jackson and Robert Smallwood (eds) *Players of Shakespeare II*, Cambridge: Cambridge University Press, 1988.

Russell Jackson and Robert Smallwood, *Players of Shakespeare III*, Cambridge: Cambridge University Press, 1993.

(The above three volumes by actors describing the roles they have played with the Royal Shakespeare Company are strongly recommended to able students as well as to teachers.)

John Russell Brown, *Shakespeare's Plays in Performance*, NY: Applause Theatre Books, 1993.

James R Bulman, (ed) *Shakespeare, Theory and Performance*, London: Routledge, 1996.

Penny Gay, *As She Likes It: Shakespeare's Unruly Women*, London: Routledge, 1994.

Andrew Gurr, *The Shakespearian Stage*, Cambridge: Cambridge University Press, 1992, 3rd edition.

Peter Holland, *English Shakespeares*, Cambridge: Cambridge University Press, 1997.

Dennis Kennedy, *Looking at Shakespeare*, Cambridge: Cambridge University Press , 1993.

Keith Parson and Pamela Mason, *Shakespeare in Performance*, London: Salamander, 1995.

Peter Reynolds *Shakespeare: Text Into Performance*, Harmondsworth: Penguin 1991.

Carol Rutter (ed) *Clamorous Voices: Shakespeare's Women Today*, London: The Women's Press 1988.

Text and Performance Series published by MacMillan Books, (1990-):
> Michael Scott, *Antony and Cleopatra*
> Peter Davison, *Hamlet*
> T F Wharton, *Henry IV, Parts 1 and 2*
> Gamini Salgado, *King Lear*
> Gordon Williams, *Macbeth*
> Bill Overton, *Merchant of Venice*
> Roger Warren, *Midsummer Night's Dream*
> Pamela Mason, *Much Ado About Nothing*
> Martin Wine, *Othello*
> Lois Potter, *Twelfth Night*

Shakespeare in Performance Series (Manchester University Press, 1987):
> Jill Levenson, *Romeo and Juliet*
> Anthony Howard, *A Midsummer Night's Dream*
> Richard Proudfoot, *Measure for Measure*
> Graham Holderness, *The Taming of the Shrew*

Teaching Shakespeare

R Adams (ed) *Teaching Shakespeare*, London: Robert Royce, 1985.

Lesley Aers and Nigel Wheale (eds) *Shakespeare in the Changing Curriculum*, London: Routledge 1991.

H R Coursen, *Teaching Shakespeare with Film and Television*, NY: Greenwood Press, 1997

James Davis and Ronald Salomone (eds) *Teaching Shakespeare Today*, Urbana, Ill: NCTE, 1993.

Rex Gibson (ed) *Secondary School Shakespeare*, Cambridge: Cambridge Institute of Education 1991.

Rex Gibson, *Shakespeare's Language* (photocopiable worksheets), Cambridge University Press, 1997.

Rex Gibson, *Teaching Shakespeare*, Cambridge: Cambridge University Press, 1998.

Susan Leach, *Shakespeare in the Classroom*, Buckingham: Open University Press 1992.

R Little, P Redsell and E Wilcox (eds), *The Shakespearian File*, London: Heinemann 1987.

Robert Livesey, *Creating with Shakespeare*, Ontario: Little Brick Schoolhouse.
Exploring Shakespeare Series, Oxford, 1994:
Susan Leach, *Romeo and Juliet*.
Brenda Pinder, *Julius Caesar*.
Bernadette Fitzgerald, *A Midsummer Night's Dream*.

David Mallick, *How Tall Is This Ghost, John?*, Adelaide: AATE 1984.

Bronwyn Mellor, *Reading Hamlet*, Scarborough, WA: Chalkface, 1989.

Wendy Michaels, *Playbuilding Shakespeare*, Melbourne: Cambridge University Press, 1996.

Peggy O'Brien (ed) *Shakespeare Set Free*, NY: Washington Square Press, 1993-5.
i. Teaching *Romeo and Juliet*, *Macbeth* and *A Midsummer Night's Dream*
ii. Teaching *Hamlet* and *Henry IV, Part 1*
iii. Teaching *Twelfth Night* and *Othello*.

Veronica O'Brien *Teaching Shakespeare*, London: Arnold, 1982.

Brenda Pinder, *Shakespeare: An Action Approach*, London: Unwin Hyman 1990.

Peter Reynolds, *Practical Approaches to Teaching Shakespeare*, Oxford: Oxford University Press 1991.

Mary Ann Rygiel, *Shakespeare Among Schoolchildren*, Urbana, Ill.: NCTE, 1992.

Peter Thomas, *Shakespeariences* Sheffield: NATE, 1998.

Student Reading

Myra Barrs (ed) *Shakespeare Superscribe*, Harmondsworth: Penguin 1980.

John Russell Brown, *Shakespeare and His Theatre*, London: Viking, 1993.

Sandy Brownjohn and Gareth Gwyn-Jones *Spotlight on Shakespeare*, London: Hodder and Stoughton 1992 (for younger students).

Wilfried Brusch, *Discovering Shakespeare*, Stuttgart: Klett, 1996.

Anna Claybourne and Rebecca Treays, *The World of Shakespeare*, London: Usborne, 1996.

Leon Garfield *Shakespeare Stories*, London: Gollancz 1988 (two volumes).

Leon Garfield, *Shakespeare: The Animated Tales* London: Heinemann, 1994 Julius Caesar (twelve volumes, based on the Russian/BBC series of animated films).

Wendy Greenhill, *Shakespeare's Theatre*, London: Heinemann, 1995.

Francois Laroque, *The Age of Shakespeare*, NY: Abrams, 1993.

Brian McFarlane, *Viewpoints on Shakespeare*, Melbourne: Longman Cheshire, 1990.

Recommended Editions of the Plays

Except where the plays are being studied for external examinations at Year 12 level, the following editions are the ones we would recommend for class use:
Cambridge School Shakespeare
Harcourt Brace School Shakespeare
Oxford School Shakespeare
Edward Arnold Student Shakespeare Series.

Other

Andrew Brownfoot, *High Fashion in Shakespeare's Time*, Stradbroke: Arquin Publication.

Audrey Ellis, *The Magpie History of Food*, London: Pan, 1977.

Madeleine Cosman *Fabulous Feasts*, New York: Braziller 1976.

Playing Shakespeare: The game of charades where every man must play a part, Oxford: Oxford Games Ltd.

THE SHAKESPEARE WORKSHOP SERIES

See our web site: www.stclairpress.com.au

This set of **PHOTOCOPIABLE** publications provides abundant opportunities for students to work together towards a thorough, complex and personal understanding of the plays as both theatre and literary texts. Each provides details of challenging activities that can be easily copied and given to students and will help students to achieve a multiplicity of interpretations of each play. The activities will stimulate wide ranging discussions and debate.

A Dagger of the Mind: Macbeth *for Senior Students* - Brenda Pinder — ISBN 0 949898 52 X

A Skirmish of Wit: **Much Ado About Nothing** - Gregory Seach — ISBN 0 949898 40 6

A Workshop Approach to **Hamlet** - Brenda Pinder & Ken Watson — ISBN 0 949898 20 1

Bitter Bread: **Richard II** *and* **The Winter's Tale** -
Catherine Radcliffe, David Nicholson and Ken Watson — ISBN 0 949898 80 5

Creative Work Ideas for **Macbeth** - Mike Hayhoe — ISBN 0 949898 01 8

Full Fathom Five: **The Tempest** - Brenda Pinder — ISBN 0 949898 24 4

Gaze on Cleopatra: **Antony and Cleopatra** - Wendy Michaels — ISBN 0 949898 32 5

Let Him Look to His Bond: **The Merchant of Venice** - Gregory Seach — ISBN 0 949898 26 0

Love's Keen Arrows: **As You Like It** - Dennis Robinson and Ken Watson — ISBN 0 949898 88 0

Moonshine Revellers: **Merry Wives of Windsor** -
Michael Kindler & Andrew Lasartes — ISBN 0 949898 83 X

Sharper Than A Serpent's Tooth: **King Lear** - Brenda Pinder — ISBN 0 949898 23 6

Some By Virtue Fall: **Measure for Measure** - Wayne Sawyer — ISBN 0 949898 63 5

Star-Cross'd Lovers: **Romeo and Juliet** - Gordon Shrubb, Ken Watson — ISBN 0 949898 87 2

Such A Mad Marriage: **Taming of the Shrew** - Ken Watson — ISBN 0 949898 46 5

The Course of True Love: **A Midsummer Night's Dream** - Mark McFadden — ISBN 0 949898 41 4

The Dogs of War: **Julius Caesar** - Wendy Michaels, Ken Watson — ISBN 0 949898 28 7

The Food of Love: **Twelfth Night** - Ken Watson — ISBN 0 949898 27 9

The Green Ey'd Monster: **Othello** - Ken Watson, Stuart Wilson — ISBN 0 949898 30 9

The Theme of Honour's Tongue: **Henry IV, Part 1** - Wendy Michaels — ISBN 0 949898 22 8

To Prove A Villain: **Richard III** - Calvin Durrant — ISBN 0 949898 47 3

We Happy Few: **Henry V** - Jo-Anne Nibbs — ISBN 0 949898 33 3